ANGLO-SCOTTISH SLEEPERS

DAVID MEARA

AMBERLEY

For Richard

First published 2018

Amberley Publishing
The Hill, Stroud,
Gloucestershire, GL5 4EP

www.amberley-books.com

ISBN: 978 1 4456 7232 8 (print)
ISBN: 978 1 4456 7233 5 (ebook)

British Library Cataloguing in Publication Data.
A catalogue record for this book is available from the British Library.

Typeset in 10pt on 13pt Celeste.
Origination by Amberley Publishing.
Printed in the UK.

Contents

The Northbound London–Fort William Sleeper approaching the Cruach Snowshed between Rannoch and Corrour stations on the morning of 7 January 2010, running an hour late due to iced points. (Norman McNab)

Preface

Railways in Britain began in a haphazard fashion, with many small private railway companies being formed in the mid-nineteenth century in an opportunistic manner and only gradually being amalgamated to form more or less coherent operators, often fighting each other for territory and customers. Under the Railways Act of 1921, the majority of the railway companies in Britain were grouped into four main companies, sometimes called 'The Big Four'. The grouping took effect from 1 January 1923. The four companies were the Great Western Railway (GWR), London & North Eastern Railway (LNER), London Midland & Scottish Railway (LMS), and the Southern Railway (SR). The Big Four were finally nationalised in January 1948. Under British Railways the country was divided into six regions (Eastern, London Midland, North Eastern, Scottish, Southern and Western), whose Executive Committees were answerable to the British Transport Commission.

After further reorganisation in the 1950s, and the appointment of Ernest Marples in 1959 as Transport Minister, Dr Richard Beeching was made Chairman of the newly formed British Railways Board and produced his famous (or infamous) report, *The Reshaping of British Railways*, which closed around 5,000 miles of track and nearly 2,000 stations in an effort to make BR cost effective. Over the next thirty years the railway's fortunes rose and fell, until under John Major's government the railways were privatised and the rail network was split off from the train operating companies.

Against this turbulent background it is extraordinary that the operation of sleeper trains has survived, even in its present truncated form. But under its current operator, Serco, the future of sleeper travel between London and Scotland is secure until at least 2029, and looks set fair to be entering an era of expansion, as the nation rediscovers the attractions of 'letting the train take the strain', while on the continent of Europe sleeper services are rapidly disappearing from the timetables. One hundred and fifty years after the idea of providing sleeping accommodation on trains was first explored, the Anglo-Scottish sleeper service remains a key part of our national railway system and transport network.

Service by Night
A British Railways poster of 1955 by David Shepherd, showing a passenger express heading under the signal gantries into the darkness out of King's Cross station. (Science and Society Picture Library)

Acknowledgements

In my researches for this book I would like to thank the staff at Search Engine at the National Railway Museum in York; staff at the National Record Office in Edinburgh; Justin Hobson at Science and Society; Doug Carmichael and the Friends of the West Highland Lines; Sebastian Wormell, archivist at Harrod's Department Store; Alisdair Campbell of the Highland Railway Society; Stuart Vallis and Norman McNab for their excellent photographs; Rose Wild of *The Times*; Michael Binyon; Trish Friedemann; Tracey Salt for deciphering my handwriting and typing up the manuscript; Ken Taylor for technical help with the images; Peter MacKay and those named in the text who contributed stories about travelling on the sleepers over the years. And especially Rosemary, for her love and forbearance.

1

'The Dream Ticket': Going North

It is just after 9 p.m. in London on a warm summer's evening. The evening rush hour has passed its peak, and those who have had to stay late at the office are now hurrying home. On Euston station the concourse is emptying, the train departures becoming less frequent. But over on a far platform sits a long, impressive-looking train, with carriages in a smart blue and purple livery, mostly sleeping cars, with sitting and lounge carriages making up the total rake of sixteen. At the front is a powerful electric Class 92 locomotive ready to pull the train on the first part of its northward journey. This is the Highland Sleeper, which departs at 21.15 and arrives at Edinburgh in the early hours of the morning, where it splits into three portions – one for Aberdeen, one for Fort William and one for Inverness.

Class 92 Locomotive in Caledonian Sleeper Livery
No. 92038 in Serco Midnight Teal livery. These electric locomotives were designed to operate through the Channel Tunnel and were intended to be mixed traffic locomotives. Six owned by GBRF have been used to haul the Caledonian Sleeper between London and Scotland. (Stuart Vallis)

Sleeping cars waiting for their passengers on Platform 1 at Euston station. (Author's Collection)

This train, and its Lowland Sleeper counterpart, offers one of the last truly romantic experiences left on the mainline railway system in Britain. The other is the Night Riviera sleeper service from London Paddington to Penzance in Cornwall. The Caledonian Sleeper plies between London and Scotland every evening except Saturdays, and there is surely no better way to travel those long distances, and no more thrilling experience than being rocked gently to sleep as you head north past Crewe in darkness, to awake some hours later to the sight of moor and mountain in the Scottish Highlands.

Back on Platform 1 at Euston station the smartly suited attendants are standing by the sleeping car doors with their clipboards, which show them the list of names of those travelling to Scotland that evening. The last passengers are walking up the platform looking for their carriage number, being checked off by the attendant and asked when they would like their morning tea or breakfast. Earlier arrivals have already ensconced themselves in the lounge car, perhaps tempted by the haggis with neeps and tatties on the menu, washed down with a dram of Scotch whisky. The lounge car, with its retro 1970s decor, is the social centre of a train that otherwise encourages privacy and anonymity, each individual or couple locked away in their own compartment. Conversation over a dram can often last into the small hours as the train travels northwards at no more than 80 miles per hour, so that passengers can be rocked to sleep in comfort.

A radio programme in the *Lives in a Landscape* series broadcast on BBC Radio 4 in 2012, and called 'The Longest Commute in Britain', followed a group of travellers on the Caledonian Sleeper and talked to those who regularly used the train. From their conversations it was clear that there is a great sense of camaraderie among the regular commuters, who get to know the attendants and each other well and feel a real sense of belonging to a 'family'. Over the years romances have blossomed in the lounge car, and firm friendships have been cemented by the shared experience of this long-distance commute.

Promptly at 9.15 p.m. the electric engine pulls the train slowly from the platform and heads into the tunnels that take the lines under the north London streets, up Camden Bank, past Alexandra Palace and away towards Watford Junction.

Current Sleeper Routes

The map shows the current routes of the overnight sleeper trains between England and Scotland, travelling via the West Coast Main Line from London Euston to Glasgow and Edinburgh, with the Highland Sleepers dividing at Edinburgh and going on to Fort William, Inverness and Aberdeen, while the Lowland Sleeper divides at Carstairs. (Stuart Vallis)

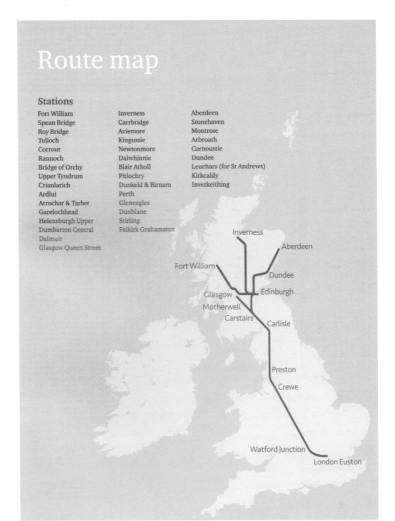

Route map

Stations

Fort William	Inverness	Aberdeen
Spean Bridge	Carrbridge	Stonehaven
Roy Bridge	Aviemore	Montrose
Tulloch	Kingussie	Arbroath
Corrour	Newtonmore	Carnoustie
Rannoch	Dalwhinnie	Dundee
Bridge of Orchy	Blair Atholl	Leuchars (for St Andrews)
Upper Tyndrum	Pitlochry	Kirkcaldy
Crianlarich	Dunkeld & Birnam	Inverkeithing
Ardlui	Perth	
Arrochar & Tarbet	Gleneagles	
Garelochhead	Dunblane	
Helensburgh Upper	Stirling	
Dumbarton Central	Falkirk Grahamston	
Dalmuir		
Glasgow Queen Street		

The lounge car quickly fills up as the train prepares to depart from Euston station. (Author's Collection)

Because of the peculiar and complicated history of railways in Britain there are now two routes to the north: the East Coast route, starting from King's Cross, and the West Coast route, which starts from Euston. Historically, there was a third route, operated by the Midland Railway, which opened the Settle and Carlisle line on 1 May 1876, thus allowing through trains to run from St Pancras in London to Glasgow (St Enoch, via Carstairs) and Edinburgh via the Waverley Route through the Scottish Borders. The East Coast route – 393 miles to Edinburgh, 47 more to Glasgow – linked together three great railway companies, the Great Northern from King's Cross to Doncaster, the North Eastern from Doncaster to Berwick-on-Tweed and the North British from Berwick to Edinburgh and Glasgow. It is a spectacular line, much better experienced in daylight, taking the traveller through the graceful curve of York station, past Durham with its magnificent cathedral, crossing the Tyne in style at Newcastle, then over the border at Berwick, following the curve of the coast and finally entering the Scottish capital deep in a valley, with Arthur's Seat and the Old Town towering above as the train pulls into Waverley Station.

The West Coast route follows the territory of the Midland Railway, later the London Midland & Scottish Railway, which combined the London & North Western Railway, several Scottish railway companies and others to form the LMS under the Railways Act of 1921. It was the largest of the railway companies and served towns and cities from London in the south to Wick in the far north of Scotland.

The grand starting point in London was St Pancras station, which was opened in 1868 by the Midland Railway as the southern terminus of its main lines to the north. The magnificent train shed by William Henry Barlow with its single-span arched roof – the largest such structure in the world at the time of its construction – was a suitably impressive starting point, fronted by the Midland Grand Hotel designed by Sir George Gilbert Scott in flamboyant Italianate Gothic style. Having perhaps spent a night in its luxurious accommodation, and done a little shopping in town, passengers boarded the sleeping carriages for the journey north. An advertisement in *Black's Tourist Guide to Scotland* of 1882 proclaims:

Advertisement for the Direct Route between Scotland and England from Glasgow (St Enoch) to London (St Pancras), via the Glasgow & South Western and Midland railways. From *Blacks Guide to Scotland*, 1882. (Author's Collection)

Right: Midland Railway Poster
An early twentieth-century poster advertising 'the most interesting route to Scotland', showing a map of the route from London St Pancras via Bedford, Nottingham, Sheffield, Leeds and the Valley of Eden route to Carlisle, where the lines divide to Glasgow or Edinburgh, and northwards to Oban, Aberdeen or Inverness and the Far North. A splendid maroon express locomotive pulls an express train of clerestory coaches, while a great black bird proudly proclaims that he is Cock o' the North. (Science and Society Picture Library)

Below: St Pancras Station
An early twentieth-century photograph showing the imposing exterior of St Pancras station and the entrance to the Midland Grand Hotel. The station opened in 1868 and the hotel in 1873. In the twenty-first century it has been magnificently restored as the departure point for Eurostar trains to the Continent. (Science and Society Picture Library)

St Pancras Station Interior, 1947
A photograph taken at a busy time of day, with mail and goods being loaded onto the trains ready for the evening departure. (Science and Society Picture Library)

Improved Sleeping Saloons (accompanied by an attendant) provided with pillows, sheets, blankets and Lavatory Accommodation, Comfortably warmed, and lighted with Gas, are run on the Night Express Trains between London and Glasgow and Perth and carriages with sleeping compartments are also run between London and Edinburgh and Greenock.

Extra charge for berths in the Sleeping Carriages is 5s in addition to the ordinary 1st Class Fare.

The southern terminus of the West Coast Main Line is now Euston station, which was first built in the 1830s by William Cubitt, and designed by Philip Hardwick. It boasted a Great Hall in the classical style, and an imposing Doric arch as the entrance on Euston Square. Tragically, all this was swept away when the station was rebuilt in a neo-brutalist style in the early 1960s. This means that passengers now have a somewhat less aesthetically pleasing experience when departing on the overnight sleeper, and there are plans to transfer sleeper operations to King's Cross while Euston is redeveloped as part of the High Speed 2 Rail Programme.

However, once aboard our train, the functional concrete cavern of Euston station can be forgotten as we settle down in our sleeping berth or sip a night-cap in the lounge car. The train passes through Watford Junction, Crewe and Preston, their empty platforms lit by great arcs of light, arriving at Carlisle around 2 a.m. and with a service stop at Edinburgh at 4.13 a.m., when the electric locomotive is exchanged for a Class 67 or 73 diesel locomotive for each of the three portions to Aberdeen, Fort William and Inverness.

While the train pounds north in the darkness, the lounge car slowly empties and passengers find their way along the narrow carpeted corridors to their berths. The Mark 3 Sleeper carriages are among the smoothest running on the network. The bed has a comfortable mattress, crisp sheets, blanket (latterly a duvet) and two pillows, with a fold-down tray and bedside light. The berths are air-conditioned and provide a wash basin

Interior of the Great Hall at Euston station. Designed by Philip Hardwick. (Science and Society Picture Library)

Corridor of a Mark 3 sleeper carriage. (Stuart Vallis)

and, in First Class, complementary toiletries. Each attendant looks after two carriages and is on hand throughout the night. As the day breaks there is a brisk knock on the door and your attendant (or steward as they used to be called) tells you where the train is on its journey and brings you your breakfast tray. Last night you pulled down your blind on the grime of London and the next morning you raise it to a view of Scottish mountains, cattle and a river valley with peaty-looking water rushing through it. If you are on the Inverness portion of the train you can follow the course of the spectacular Highland Line from Perth to Inverness. It is a particularly powerful experience to board the train at Euston amid the noise and bustle of London and to get out at, say, Kingussie, into total silence, which is only broken by the post van going by.

Some of my happiest memories of Scottish holidays as a young teenager centre around the way in which my family began the journey north to Scotland – by the night sleeper trains, which, in the 1960s, ran to over thirty destinations throughout Britain. I first travelled by sleeper in 1959, on a relief train from Euston in an old Third Class four-berth compartment, such was the demand for the service during the peak summer holiday period. We were provided only with pillows and blankets, but there was a restaurant car on the train, so we had the comparative luxury of an evening meal served in style – with crisp linen tablecloths and British Rail cutlery – before retiring to our cabin. We could sip our Brown Windsor soup and smugly watch the cars toiling up the M1 motorway as we swept smoothly northwards.

On my second journey north in 1960, I travelled on 'The Royal Highlander', which ran between London Euston and Inverness. On the carriage doors were posted the names and berth numbers of the passengers, and you would often see Lord or Lieutenant Colonel So and So travelling north to their shooting at the start of the grouse season in August. Sir Max Hastings, writer and former editor of *The Daily Telegraph*, has fond memories of travelling at this time of year:

> I grew up with the legend of catching the night sleeper to Scotland and experienced the same joy as generations of sportsmen from those wonderfully stylish trains. Never did a grimy London station seem so thrilling as when bearing us north to the hills, where we'd awaken to the sight of the heather beside the track north of Perth. A print of George Earl's painting '*Going North*' (now in the National Railway Museum) has hung on my wall for most of my life, a reminder of so many supremely happy pilgrimages to the Highlands. The grouse are still there, thank heaven, but nowadays, train windows will not open, restaurant cars are extinct and almost every shooter and fisher travels north via the boring old M6.
>
> *Country Life*, 11 September 2013

The fare in the 1960s for a Second Class sleeper was 22s 6d, and the dining car offered dinner before Crewe (13s 6d per person in 1966) and a cooked breakfast after Perth in the morning. In its day it was the longest distance through train in Britain, and took the longest journey time of about fourteen hours. In subsequent years we used the Car Sleeper Ltd between London and Perth, later re-branded as Motorail, arriving at Perth station just before 6 a.m. and enjoying a splendid Scottish breakfast in the station restaurant while waiting for the car to be unloaded. Afterwards we would set off up the A9, stopping for

Going North, 1893, by George Earl
Going North depicts the crowd of passengers at King's Cross station getting ready to board the train to Scotland for the shooting season. There is a glorious mix of social classes, from the gentry and their ladies to the servants, grooms, footmen, porters and others attending to them and their dogs. Earl was a keen sportsman who specialised in animal paintings. This painting and its companion, *Coming South*, were commissioned by Sir Andrew Barclay Walker and now hang in the National Railway Museum. The passengers are presumably awaiting the 10 a.m. departure in the East Hall of King's Cross, but it is easy to imagine them getting ready to board the night express to take them to the Highlands and their sporting estates. (Science and Society Picture Library)

coffee at Pitlochry, where we would buy supplies for a picnic lunch, and then enjoy that wonderful run to Inverness and beyond. Our destination was usually the Orkney Islands, my mother's birthplace, which took two days further travel to reach, but occasionally we would enjoy a motoring holiday in the Highlands, exploring the remote and wild delights of Sutherland. Wherever we ended up, that first night on the sleeper was an exciting prelude to Scotland and the far north, which in the days before frequent air travel seemed a long way away and a tremendous adventure.

Over the subsequent years I have travelled on all the remaining sleeper services and watched the fortunes of the service rise and fall, and then in this century rise again as we have become disenchanted with long-distance car travel or the hassle of airports and flying. As we enjoy the improvements in the service that the current operator, Serco, is introducing, and welcome the arrival of brand new rolling stock and an enhanced travelling experience from 2018 onwards, this book aims to give a brief history of how sleeper travel between England and Scotland has evolved over the past 150 years, and to conjure up something of the excitement, romance and idiosyncrasy of the sleeper service through the personal stories of those who have travelled on the sleepers.

Left: Interior of a First Class cabin on the Mark 3 sleeper. (Stuart Vallis)

Below: The northbound London to Fort William Sleeper passing through the remote Gorton loop on 1 May 2015 at 8.28 a.m., pulled by a Class 67 locomotive, *Cairn Gorm*, in the new Serco Midnight Teal livery. (Norman McNab)

2

'Travel in Your Pyjamas': A Brief History of Sleeper Travel

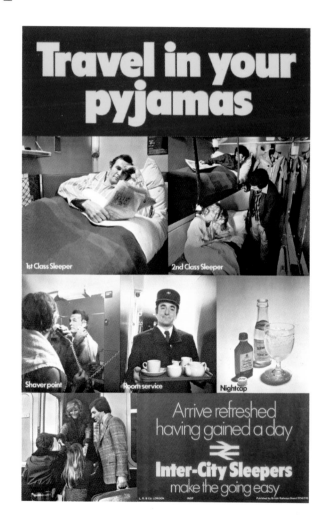

British Rail Sleeper poster of the 1970s. (Science and Society Picture Library)

'Bring your own bedding' was good advice if you were a passenger on a night train about 150 years ago. In those days not only were the carriages fairly primitive, but the idea of taking your clothes off and going to bed on a train would have seemed strange and somewhat indecent to the Victorian traveller. Before the advent of dedicated sleeping cars, passengers had to make do within the standard daytime carriages. But the Victorians were ingenious, and to mitigate the discomfort of a night spent sitting upright, Harrods department store marketed a contraption consisting of two poles with a sheet of webbing attached, which could be placed across the carriage seats. It cost 4s 9d and looks extremely uncomfortable. There were also invalid carriages in the 1850s and '60s that contained an adjustable bed and a lavatory, but they seem to have been few in number and were only available for those unable to travel in a standard carriage through illness or disability.

It was in the 1870s that the first real sleeping cars were introduced. The North British Railway commissioned a six-wheel car, built by the Ashbury Railway Carriage & Iron Company, Manchester, which consisted of a Second Class seating compartment and two First Class compartments that could be ingeniously converted into sleeping accommodation. There was also a lavatory and a water closet, and a luggage compartment

1066 **HARROD'S STORES, Limited, Brompton.**
BAGS, TRUNKS, AND PORTMANTEAUS.
No. 19 DEPARTMENT—*FIRST FLOOR.*

PEAKE'S PORTABLE SLEEPING REST

FOR

RAILWAY TRAVELLERS.

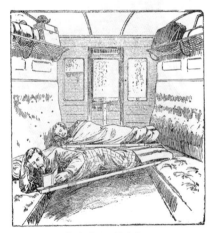

Sleeping Rest, as Illustration.
Length when folded, 36 inches. Breadth, 3½ inches.
Price, 4/9 each.

FRONT VIEW

FOLDED

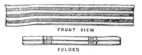

All the above are delivered Carriage free, subject to the Conditions set forth on page 4.

Peake's Portable Sleeping Rest
This device appears in the 1895 edition of the Harrod's department store catalogue, although it had been available some years previously. It was easily folded for travelling, and when opened up could be placed across the carriage seats to form a kind of precarious camp bed. The contraptions cost 4s 9d each. In the accompanying illustration the occupants look extremely uncomfortable and would have done better to lie on the upholstered seats in the compartment.
(Harrods Limited)

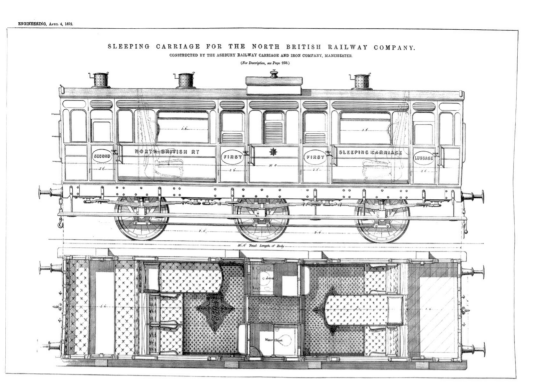

ENGINEERING, April 4, 1873.

SLEEPING CARRIAGE FOR THE NORTH BRITISH RAILWAY COMPANY.

CONSTRUCTED BY THE ASHBURY RAILWAY CARRIAGE AND IRON COMPANY, MANCHESTER.

(For Description, see Page 236.)

North British Railway Sleeping Carriage, 1873

This was the first sleeping carriage to be built, constructed by the Ashbury Railway Carriage & Iron Company, Manchester. It was 30 ft long, 6 ft 6 in. wide, and 6 ft 10 in. in height. At one end of the carriage is a Second Class compartment and at the other is a luggage compartment. The central portion consists of two First Class compartments with a lobby in between, with a lavatory and a water closet supplied with water from a tank in the roof.

The First Class compartments convert into sleeper use by folding the seat up and pulling the back forward, making a 6 ft 3 in. bed. (Science and Society Picture Library)

at the opposite end. The interior was finished in polished walnut wood with ebony and gold mountings, carpeted floors and velvet upholstery. It was attached to the 1 p.m. express train from Glasgow to King's Cross via the East Coast route on 2 April 1873, and passengers paid a sleeper supplement of 10s. Three months later the Great Northern Railway put on a similar car so that the service could operate in each direction every night. In the early days passengers were few and far between, and the sleeping cars sometimes ran empty. In the height of summer 1873 the North British Carriage averaged fewer than seven passengers a week, so it is clear that the idea took some time to catch on.

Soon the service spread to the West Coast route, where the LNWR had been urged since 1871 to build sleeping carriages. In 1873 two modified saloons were introduced as an experiment, and from 1 October were attached to the 8.40 p.m. mail train to Glasgow. Further carriages were introduced on the London to Glasgow service, with various modifications, and in 1881 two new carriages, based on the wagons-lits in use on the Belgian Railways, were built, with accommodation for four men and two ladies, with adjoining lavatories and a vestibule fitted with moveable chairs and a coke stove, for use as a smoking lounge.

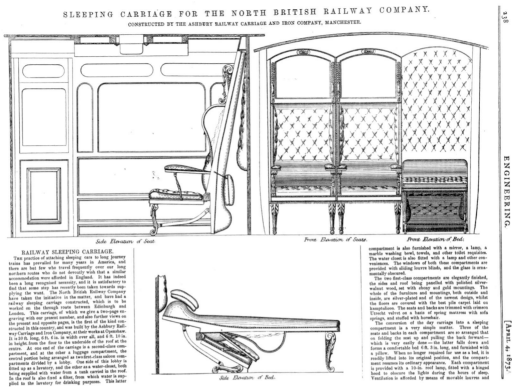

SLEEPING CARRIAGE FOR THE NORTH BRITISH RAILWAY COMPANY.

CONSTRUCTED BY THE ASHBURY RAILWAY CARRIAGE AND IRON COMPANY, MANCHESTER.

Side Elevation of Seat.

Front Elevation of Seats.

Front Elevation of Bed.

Side Elevation of Bed.

RAILWAY SLEEPING CARRIAGE.

THE practice of attaching sleeping cars to long journey trains has prevailed for many years in America, and there are but few who travel frequently over our long northern routes who do not devoutly wish that a similar accommodation were afforded in England. It has indeed been a long recognised necessity, and it is satisfactory to find that some step has recently been taken towards supplying the want. The North British Railway Company have taken the initiative in the matter, and have had a railway sleeping carriage constructed, which is to be worked on the through route between Edinburgh and London. This carriage, of which we give a two-page engraving with our present number, and also further views on the present and opposite pages, is the first of the kind constructed in this country, and was built by the Ashbury Railway Carriage and Iron Company, at their works at Openshaw. It is 30 ft. long, 6 ft. 6 in. in width over all, and 6 ft. 10 in. in height from the floor to the underside of the roof at the centre. At one end of the carriage is a second-class compartment, and at the other a luggage compartment, the central portion being arranged as two first-class saloon compartments divided by a lobby. One side of this lobby is fitted up as a lavatory, and the other as a water-closet, both being supplied with water from a tank carried in the roof. In the roof is also fixed a filter, from which water is supplied to the lavatory for drinking purposes. This latter compartment is also furnished with a mirror, a lamp, a marble washing bowl, towels, and other toilet requisites. The water closet is also fitted with a lamp and other conveniences. The windows of both these compartments are provided with sliding louvre blinds, and the glass is ornamentally obscured.

The two first-class compartments are elegantly finished, the sides and roof being panelled with polished silver-walnut wood, set with ebony and gold mountings. The whole of the furniture and mountings, both outside and inside, are silver-plated and of the newest design, whilst the floors are covered with the best pile carpet laid on kamptulicon. The seats and backs are trimmed with crimson Utrecht velvet on a basis of spring mattress with sofa springs, and stuffed with horsehair.

The conversion of the day carriage into a sleeping compartment is a very simple matter. Three of the seats and backs in each compartment are so arranged that on folding the seat up and pulling the back forward—which is very easily done—the latter falls down and forms a comfortable bed 6 ft. 3 in. long, and furnished with a pillow. When no longer required for use as a bed, it is readily lifted into its original position, and the compartment resumes its ordinary appearance. Each compartment is provided with a 10-in. roof lamp, fitted with a hinged hood to obscure the lights during the hours of sleep. Ventilation is afforded by means of movable louvres and

North British Railway Sleeping Carriage, 1873
Side elevation of seat and bed. (Science and Society Picture Library)

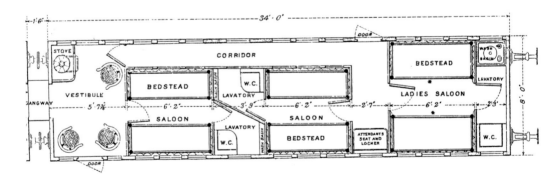

LNWR Sleeping Saloon, 1881
These sleeping cars were coupled in pairs with a flexible gangway in between. Each provided sleeping berths for four men and two ladies in three compartments, each with an adjoining lavatory. They included a vestibule with moveable chairs and a coke stove, which provided the heating. There was also a side corridor connecting to the vestibule, allowing greater privacy. (Science and Society Picture Library)

Meanwhile the Midland Railway began to introduce American-built Pullman sleeping cars in 1874. These were the brainchild of George Mortimer Pullman, who had designed and built the first luxury sleeping car, named *Pioneer*, in 1864 at a cost of $20,000 and at his own expense. The day seats were adapted to make comfortable beds and the upper berths were raised against the roof when not in use. Linen bedding and pillows were provided, and the heating and lighting were of a superior standard. The interior was finished in polished black walnut, the washstands were marble and the floor was carpeted.

This luxurious travelling accommodation was unknown in England until James Allport, General Manager of the Midland Railway, decided to pay a visit to America in the autumn of 1872 to see these new carriages for himself. He travelled 6,000 miles over the American network, much of it in Pullman's parlour and sleeping cars. He was so impressed that on his return he persuaded his directors to invite George Pullman over to England. Pullman offered to build cars of equal luxury suitable for the British loading gauge, to ship them to England and to cover the operational costs in return for a 'Pullman Supplement', for a period of fifteen years. The agreement was signed on 18 February 1873 and by the end of the year the component parts were arriving from Detroit at the Midland Railway's headquarters at Derby. By 21 January 1874 the first sleeping car, named *Midland*, had been completed. It was 58 ft 9 in. long and 8 ft 9 in. wide with end observation platforms and a clerestory roof, and bogies of the American type.

Inside there were ten sections comprising pairs of longitudinal seats facing each other that could be converted into beds, and upper berths that could be lowered on pulleys for night-time use. There were also two private state-rooms, and at either end of the carriage a ladies' and a gentlemen's toilet and water closet. The interior was lit by kerosene lamps suspended from the centre of the clerestory roof, and it was heated by radiators fed by a hot water system.

On 15 February 1874 the second Pullman car, *Excelsior*, was completed and then the first 'parlour' car, *Victoria*, which was fitted with seventeen individual armchairs, mounted on pivots and upholstered in moquette, at a total cost of £3,000.

The first scheduled service began on 1 June 1874 between Bradford and London St Pancras, arriving at 2.05 p.m. and returning as a sleeping car service at midnight.

Interior of a Midland Railway Pullman sleeping car showing the bunks in the raised position. (Science and Society Picture Library)

Interior of Midland Pullman Sleeping Car
Part of the interior of 1900 Pullman sleeper
No. 36, showing a wash basin area with
the lavatory beyond. The decoration is
ornate, but the curtains offer little privacy.
The vehicle was altered to private berths
throughout in 1905. (Science and Society
Picture Library)

In spite of criticism about the increased weight and cost of Pullman trains, as well as a dislike of the open saloon style of the carriages, further sleeping cars were built over the next three years, and the service was boosted when the Midland direct route to Scotland was opened via the Settle and Carlisle Line into Glasgow (St Enoch) in 1876. Soon sleepers were also running to Edinburgh.

The superior comfort and novelty value of these American-style cars inspired one Scottish gentleman to hire a private train consisting of an engine, a drawing room car and a sleeping car to take his party of intrepid fellow travellers on a novel holiday trip around the Scottish Highlands in 1876. It clearly took an immense amount of trouble to organise and must have given the various railway companies quite a headache while the little train toured their networks.

When the agreement with Pullman expired in 1888 the Midland Railway began designing their own sleeping cars, and removed the Pullman name from existing stock. In 1899 an order was placed for the last four Pullman sleeping cars at a cost of £3,495 each, and they entered service in April 1900. These were rebuilt in 1905 with private berths throughout, and three of the cars survived to be taken over by the London Midland & Scottish Railway Company at its formation in 1923.

Gradually the Pullman cars were phased out completely, finding alternative uses or languishing in sidings until they fell apart. But they had set a standard that was to become the benchmark for subsequent sleeper design, even though later generations of sleepers were more utilitarian and less luxurious in finish.

T. G. Clayton, the Midland Carriage Superintendent, had been working on a carriage design of his own, including the American-style bogie suspension and traditional compartment-style passenger accommodation. By the winter of 1875 Clayton built the first British passenger carriages on two six-wheel bogies. Each carriage was 54 ft long – a huge increase in size from the old six-wheelers. So, in 1876 the Midland Railway began

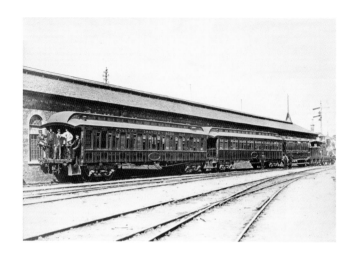

The Pullman Picnic Train, 1876. (Science and Society Picture Library)

its Anglo-Scottish services with stock that was considerably in advance of its rivals. This was important as the Midland's route was longer than those of the other companies, and consequently they had to attract customers by providing a superior level of service.

Hot and cold running water was provided in their carriages by the London & North Western Railway in 1882, and en suite lavatories became a feature of First Class compartments. The first sleeping carriage with transverse berths opening onto a side corridor was built for the North Eastern Railway in 1894, designed by David Bain, and this arrangement has become the norm ever since. This change from the longitudinal to the transverse sleeping position did not please everyone at the time, and can still feel strange. In the twentieth century the disorientating experience of transverse travel has been captured by the poet Norman MacCaig in his poem 'Sleeping Compartment', in which he complains of being carried sideways 'like a timber broadside in a fast stream', and concludes with the lovely line, 'I draw in my feet to let Aviemore pass.'

Nevertheless, over 100 years ago the die was cast, and sleeper beds have been placed transversely to the line of travel ever since.

To understand the context of the evolution of sleeping car design, we need to remember the rivalry that existed between the railway companies who ran trains over the East Coast route and the West Coast route. The origins of the West Coast Main Line through Cumbria go back to the 1830s, when a railway through to Scotland was seen as the logical extension of the trunk routes from London to the north. The Lancaster & Carlisle Railway, formed in 1843, joined with other partners to create the 69 miles of track between Lancaster and Carlisle. With the completion of the Caledonian Railway from Carlisle to Glasgow and Edinburgh in 1848, the West Coast route was opened between London and Scotland, two years ahead of their East Coast rivals. The journey took twelve and a half hours without the need to change trains, and the Post Office promptly switched its London–Edinburgh mail traffic from the East Coast to the West Coast route.

Further destinations became possible with the opening of the Forth Bridge in 1890. This massive cantilevered structure, designed by Sir John Fowler and Sir Benjamin Baker, and built by Tancred, Arrol & Co. between 1882 and 1890, was 1½ miles long and weighed over 51,000 tonnes. Built of steel, with granite piers and viaducts, the bridge was financed by a

James Caird's Picnic Party

A Scottish gentleman, James Caird, organised a travelling holiday in 1876, which a contemporary newspaper called 'The Pullman Picnic Party'. With the co-operation of the railway authorities and the use of two Pullman Cars the party of sixteen people, including two maid servants, a cook and a steward, travelled for twenty-six days in a sleeping car and a drawing room car through the Lowlands of Scotland, across the Forth Bridge and on the Highland Railway as far as Wick. They returned along the West Coast, concluding their excursion with a run over the Settle and Carlisle line en route back to London St Pancras.

The expedition was the brainchild of one man, who kept the route secret from his companions. The party travelled at slower speeds so that they could enjoy the scenery better, and on the Highland Railway portion were accompanied by half a dozen navvies to ensure the cars cleared the low bridges, as the rails had to be lowered, in one case by 6 inches, to permit them to pass. Cooking arrangements were primitive, and dinners usually consisted of cold collations. The newspaper report concluded: 'The Pullman car picnic party has shown that you may travel for a month with perfect enjoyment by a very slight modification of existing arrangements...' (Science and Society Picture Library)

Midland Railway Pullman Sleeping Car No. 36 One of the last Pullman sleeping cars to be delivered to the Midland Railway, which entered service in April 1900. Designed by George Mortimer Pullman (1831–97), an American engineer who invented the Pullman Sleeping Car. (Science and Society Picture Library)

Midland Railway four-wheel bogie sleeping carriage, built 1887. (Science and Society Picture Library)

consortium of the North British Railway, the Midland Railway, the North Eastern Railway and the Great Northern Railway, all of whom stood to benefit from the direct link to the Highlands and Aberdeen.

The West Coast route from Euston to Aberdeen was 540 miles, while the East Coast route was only 523 miles. The intense rivalry between the companies resulted in what became known as the 'Races to the North'. The tensions involved are well summed up in the following account:

The competition reached a climax in 1895 when a new night express was introduced on the East Coast Line. Trains left Euston and King's Cross simultaneously at 8 pm, but the East Coast train arrived in Aberdeen at 7.20 am, twenty minutes ahead of the rival ... Then on 15th July the West Coast, without warning, accelerated its 8 pm from Euston to give a 7 am arrival in Aberdeen. Telegrams flashed between the East Coast general managers in London, York and Edinburgh. The result was that from 22nd July the 8 pm from King's Cross was timed to reach Aberdeen at 6.45 am.

A Regional History of the Railways of Great Britain: Vol 15: North of Scotland:
John Thomas and David Turnock: p. 159

⚜ SLEEPING CARRIAGES. ⚜

SLEEPING CARRIAGES, provided with sheets, rugs, &c., and fitted with separate lavatories for ladies and gentlemen, are attached to the undermentioned trains. The charge is 5s. per berth, in addition to first class railway fares.

Stations.	Weekdays.							Sundays.				
	A B		A		A	C		D				
King's Cross ..dep	7 45 p.m.	8 15 p.m.	8 45 p.m.	10 30 p.m.	11 30 p.m.	11 30 p.m.	11 45 p.m.	7 45 p.m.	8 15 p.m.	8 45 p.m.	11 30 p.m.	11 45 p.m.
York .... "	11 27 "	11 57 "	1 15 a.m.	3 35 a.m.	3 12 a.m.	3 12 a.m.	3 27 a.m.	11 27 "	11 57 "	1 15 a.m.	3 12 a.m.	3 27 a.m.
Newcastle .... "	1 7 a.m.	1 32 a.m.	3 10 "	6 0 "	4 47 "	4 47 "	5 7 "*‡	1 7 a.m.	1 32 a.m.	3 10 "	4 47 "	5 7 "‡
Edinburgh .... arr	3 30 "	4 0 "	5 55 "	8f58 "*	7 15 "	7 15 "	7 30 "	3 30 "	4 0 "	5 55 "	7 15 "*‡	7 30 "‡
Glasgow ...... "	—	5 35 "	7e23 "*‡	—	—	—	8h50 "*	—	5 35 "	7 23 "‡	—	8 50 "‡
Aberdeen ...... "	—	7 20 "	—	—	11 10 "*‡	11 20 "*‡	—	—	7 20 "*‡	—	11 10 "*‡	—
Perth .... "	4g40 "	5 14 "	—	—	8 55 "*‡	8 40 "*‡	—	4 40 "	5 14 "	—	8 55 "*	—
Inverness ...... "	8g35 "*	9 10 "*‡	—	—	—	—	—	8 35 "*	9 10 "*‡	—	—	—
Fort William .. "	—	9 43 "*‡	—	—	—	—	—	—	9 43 "*‡	—	—	—

A—Saturdays excepted. B—Will run from 7th July to 8th August. C—Saturdays only. D—Will only run on 16th August. e—On Sunday mornings is due at Glasgow at 7.30. f—Runs to Berwick only on Sunday mornings. g—From 21st July to 8th August. h—On Sunday mornings arrives at Glasgow at 10.43.
*—Through car from King's Cross terminating at this point.

‡ Corridor Sleeping Carriage with Transverse Berths, accompanied by an attendant who provides tea, coffee, &c.

Stations.	Weekdays.				Sundays.	
Fort William dep	—	—	4 20 p.m.*‡	5 30 p.m.*‡	4 10 p.m.	—
Inverness ...... "	—	—	—	9 40 "*‡	—	—
Perth ...... "	—	7 55 p.m.*‡	—	9 40 "*‡	4 10 p.m.	—
Aberdeen ...... "	3 30 p.m.	—	—	7 45 "*‡	3 30 "	—
Glasgow ...... "	6 0 "*‡	—	—	—	5 0 "*	9 35 p.m.*‡
Edinburgh ...... "	7 45 "	9 40 "*‡	10 50 "*‡	11 15 "	7 45 "	11 0 "*‡
Newcastle ...... "	a11 15 "*‡	12 37 a.m.	1 34 a.m.	1 49 a.m.	11 15 "*‡	2 0 a.m.
York ...... arr	1 15 a.m.	2 22 "	3 15 "	3 29 "	1 12 a.m.	3 45 "
King's Cross "	5 50 "	6 40 "	7 10 "	7 35 "	5 50 "	8 5 "

a—The car which starts from Newcastle does not run on Saturday nights.   *—Through car between this point and King's Cross.

‡ Corridor Sleeping Carriage with Transverse Berths, accompanied by an attendant who provides tea, coffee, &c.

BERTHS CAN BE SECURED IN ADVANCE

By giving notice to the Great Northern Company's Superintendent at KING'S CROSS; the North Eastern Company's Chief Passenger Agent at YORK; the North British Company's Superintendent at EDINBURGH, and at the East Coast Companies' Offices, 16, South St. Andrew Street, EDINBURGH; 37, West George Street, GLASGOW; General Station, PERTH; 26, Market Street, ABERDEEN; and 4, Academy Street, INVERNESS; or by giving notice to the Station-masters at any station at which the express trains call, between London, Edinburgh, Glasgow, Perth, Aberdeen, and Inverness.

In ordering berths passengers should state whether required for lady or gentleman.

Passengers travelling in the Sleeping Carriages by the up trains arriving at King's Cross at 5.50 a.m., 6.40 a.m., and 7.10 a.m., and by the down train arriving at Newcastle at 5.0 a.m., may remain in them until 8.0 a.m.

SUPPLY OF RUGS AND PILLOWS TO PASSENGERS BY NIGHT EXPRESS TRAINS.—Rugs and Pillows are supplied for first and third class passengers, in the through East Coast Trains, travelling to and from Stations south of, and including Edinburgh, Glasgow, Perth, and Aberdeen, at a charge of 6d. per Rug, and 6d. per Pillow.

North Eastern Railway Timetable 1902
The timetable shows the trains with sleeping carriages between King's Cross, Inverness and Fort William in 1902. A note informs passengers that the sleeping carriages now have corridors and transverse berths. (Science and Society Picture Library)

After this passenger safety and convenience were forgotten, and speed restrictions were ignored. Newspaper reporters followed and egged on the contest, and a potential disaster was only averted when a NBR chief inspector travelling to Aberdeen was horrified that speed limits were broken on both the Forth and Tay bridges, and called a halt to the races. The general managers had learnt their lesson and resolved not to allow speed to trump safety or passenger comfort again. Henceforth the timetable was king, and generous timings were maintained long after more powerful locomotives made higher speeds quite safe. The rivalries were only resumed in the 1920s between the LMS and the LNER, with both companies competing for speed and luxury over these now well-established routes.

By 1914 sleeper services were well established on all trunk routes from London to Scotland. Carriages offered single and double cabins, hot and cold water, electric lighting and fans.

A typical example was the West Coast Joint Stock vehicle with ten berths, a lavatory at one end, a smoking compartment and an attendant's cubicle at the other end. A lockable connecting door between each pair of berths allowed them to be converted into two-bedroom suites. Passengers could order refreshments from the attendant, and north of Perth or

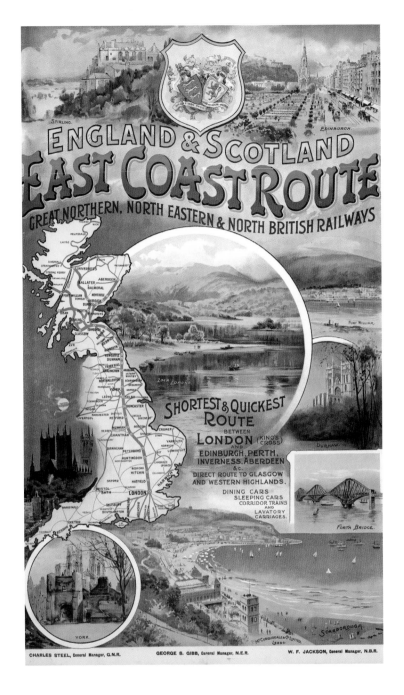

East Coast Route between England and Scotland

This early poster shows a map of the route run by the Great Northern, North Eastern and North British railways between London King's Cross and Edinburgh, Perth, Inverness and Aberdeen. It advertises 'Dining Cars, Sleeping Cars, Corridor Trains and Lavatory Carriages' and is illustrated with views of York, Scarborough, Lincoln, Durham, the Forth Bridge, Loch Lomond, Fort William, Stirling and Edinburgh, with the arms of Scotland and England entwined at the top. (Science and Society Picture Library)

THE FORTH BRIDGE

LONDON AND NORTH EASTERN RAILWAY OF ENGLAND AND SCOTLAND

Forth Bridge Poster
This poster was designed by Henry George Gawthorn (1879–1941), who produced several posters for the LNER. It shows an express train crossing the Forth Bridge, opened in 1890 to connect the East Coast Route between London and Aberdeen. (Science and Society Picture Library)

Aberdeen breakfast could be taken at station refreshment rooms, or food baskets could be put on the train.

The Highland Railway timetable for October 1915 advertised the following at Kinguissie:

> Hot Luncheon or Dinner Basket (with Small Bottle of Claret) 3s; Breakfast and Tea Baskets (one Hot Course) 2s 6d, can be had on receipt of a telegram, sent Free by the Attendants on the Train from a previous stopping station. Plain Tea or Breakfast 1s. Cold Luncheon Baskets, with Small Bottle of Claret, Bottle of Ale, Mineral Water 3s. Tea and Light Refreshments are brought to the trains.
>
> Quoted in *The Skye and Dingwall Railway*: Peter Tatlow

Soon a Pullman car was added so that meals could be taken on the train north of Perth.

In 1923 Sir Nigel Gresley was appointed Chief Mechanical Engineer at LNER, and he and his team exercised a significant influence on carriage design. His assistant Carriage & Wagon

EAST COAST "EXPRESS" ROUTE.
GREAT NORTHERN AND NORTH-EASTERN RAILWAYS.

SPECIAL EXPRESS TRAINS
BETWEEN
LONDON AND EDINBURGH AND GLASGOW.

LONDON TO EDINBURGH IN 9.0 HRS.   TO GLASGOW IN 10 HRS. 20 MINS.

ADDITIONAL SPECIAL EXPRESS TRAINS
Now run between Glasgow, Edinburgh, and London, as under :

DOWN.		UP.	
KING'S CROSS ...... Dep. 10.0 A.M.		GLASGOW........ Dep. 8.40 A.M.
EDINBURGH .... Arr. 7.0 P.M.		EDINBURGH........ ,, 10.0 ,,
GLASGOW............ ,, 8.20 ,,		KING'S CROSS ...... Arr. 7.0 P.M.

THROUGH WEEK-DAY SERVICE
BETWEEN LONDON AND SCOTLAND BY EAST COAST ROUTE.

DOWN.					UP.				
	A.M.	A.M.	α P.M.	P.M.	P.M.		A.M.	P.M.	A.M.	P.M.	A.M.
KING'S Cross,Dep.	10.0	10.35	8.0*	8.30*	9.0	WICK ...... Dep.	12.10	..	11.30	11.30	..
Edinburgh ..Arr.	7.0	8.88	5.30	6.0	7.20	Thurso .... ,,	12.25	..	11.40	11.40	..
Glasgow...... ,,	8.20	10.25	7.37	7.37	8.58	Helmsdale.. ,,	3.30	6.0	2.10	2.10	..
Stirling...... ,,	8.25	10.27	6.59	7.28	8.43	Golspie .... ,,	4.30	7.0	2.50	2.50	..
Perth ...... ,,	9.35	11.40	8.0	8.23	9.55	Inverness.. ,,	10.10	1.30	10.0†	10.0†	..
Dundee .... ,,	10.30	12.50	9.35	9.38	12.0	Aberdeen .. ,,	12.30	4.40	..	..	8.55
Aberdeen .... ,,	3.20	3.20	..	11.40	2.15	Dundee.... ,,	4.0	6.45	7.0	11.10	
Inverness.... ,,	8.0	8.0	..	1.30	6.25	Perth...... ,,	4.20	7.35	7.30	12.0	
Golspie...... ,,	1.17	1.17	..	5.14	..	Stirling .... ,,	5.19	8.41	8.41	1.5	
Helmsdale .. ,,	2.10	2.10	..	5.51	..	Glasgow.... ,,	6.0	8.50	8.40	1.0	
Thurso...... ,,	4.45	4.45	..	7.50	..	Edinburgh.. ,,	7.30	10.20	10.0	10.15	2.50
Wick........ ,,	5.0	5.0	..	8.0	..	KING'S Cross,Ar.	5.45	8.15	7.0	8.40	8.0

Third Class tickets are issued by all trains, except the additional Special Scotch Express trains from King's Cross at 10.0 A.M., and Edinburgh at 10.0 A.M.

α The 8.0 P.M. train from King's Cross will be run from Monday, 2d July, to Friday, 17th August, inclusive, Saturdays and Sundays excepted.

* The 8.0 and 8.30 P.M. Express trains from King's Cross are in direct connection with the "Iona" and other West Coast Steamers.

† Not run from Inverness on Saturday nights.

IMPROVED CARRIAGE STOCK
has been constructed, and is now in use, for through traffic between London and Scotland.
PULLMAN CARS & SLEEPING CARRIAGES
are attached to the night trains.

Alterations may be made in the times of the trains from month to month, for particulars of which see the East Coast Railways' Monthly Time Books.

Conductors in charge of through luggage travel with the Express trains leaving London at 10.0 and 10.35 A.M., 8.0, 8.30, and 9.0 P.M.; and Perth at 4.20 P.M. and 7.30 A.M.; and Edinburgh at 10.0, 10.15 A.M., 7.30 P.M. and 10.20 P.M.

Advertisements for the East Coast Route between England and Scotland from *Black's Guide to Scotland* 1882. (Author's Collection)

LONDON & NORTH-WESTERN AND CALEDONIAN RAILWAYS
WEST COAST ROYAL MAIL ROUTE
BETWEEN
ENGLAND AND SCOTLAND.

1st, 2d, and 3d CLASS TOURIST TICKETS,

Available from the date of issue, up to and including the 31st December 1883, are (during the Season commencing 1st May) issued from all Principal Stations in England to the chief places of interest in Scotland, and also from the same places in Scotland to English Stations.

Passengers by the Through Trains between London (Euston Station) and Scotland are conveyed in
THROUGH CARRIAGES
of the most improved description, and constructed specially for the accommodation of this Traffic.

Saloons, Family Carriages, Reserved Compartments, and all other conveniences necessary to ensure comfort on the journey, can be arranged upon application to Mr. G. P. NEELE, Superintendent of the L. and N.-W. Line, Euston Station, London; Mr. IRVINE KEMPT, General Superintendent of the Caledonian Railway, Glasgow; or to any of the Stationmasters at the Stations on the West Coast Route.

By the opening of the line of Railway from CALLANDER to OBAN direct Railway communication is afforded by the West Coast Route to Loch Awe, Taynuilt, and Oban. Steamers sail in connection to and from Iona, Staffa, and the Western Islands.

TABLE OF EXPRESS TRAINS BETWEEN LONDON AND SCOTLAND.
DOWN JOURNEY.

STATIONS.		WEEK DAYS.						SUNDAYS.	
		morn.	morn.	morn.	morn.	night.	night.	night.	night.
London (Euston) .	dep.	5.15	7.15	10.0	11.0	8.50	9.0	8.50	9.0
Edinburgh (Princes St. Stn.)	arr.	4.30	5.50	8.0	9.45	6.45	7.50	6.45	7.50
Glasgow (Central Station)	,,	4.45	6.0	8.0	10.0	6.55	8.0	6.55	8.0
Greenock .	,,	5.49	7.15	9.5	11.42	*7.50	*9·46	7.50	9.46
Stirling .	,,	5.39	..	8.25	10.27	7.21	*8.43	7.21	8.43
Oban .	,,	10.0	..	..	4.35	*12.27	..	12.27	..
Perth .	,,	6.50	..	9.35	11.40	8.15	*9.55	8.15	9.55
Aberdeen .	,,	10.10	..	..	3.20	11.40	*2.15	11.40	2.15
Inverness .	,,	..	..	..	8.0	1.30	*6.25	1.30	6.25

No connection from London to Places marked thus (*) on Saturday Nights.
Additional Trains will be run during the months of June, July, August, and September

Advertisement for the West Coast Route between England and Scotland, showing two night departures from London Euston to Perth, Aberdeen and Inverness. From *Black's Guide to Scotland* 1882. (Author's Collection)

Superintendent was Oliver Bulleid, and together they introduced a range of developments in LNER sleeping cars, ranging from a refined heating and ventilation system, a special Bulleid-designed coathanger and simplified interior decor that was neat and functional. The coathanger was particularly clever as it enabled you to hang up your jacket first, and then hang your trousers on a bar that projected beyond the jacket support – a logical and practical solution when a gentleman was undressing for bed in a confined space. Demand for sleeping accommodation grew rapidly during the 1920s, but the commercial managers were reluctant to jeopardise their lucrative First Class business by introducing cheaper Third Class accommodation. However, in May 1928 sixteen Third Class cars were built with seven four-berth compartments and a lavatory at each end of the coach. Passengers were provided with pillows and blankets for a 7 shilling supplement to the Third Class fare.

The poet T. S. Eliot clearly enjoyed the experience of sleeper travel in the 1920s and early 1930s, reflected in his poem 'Skimbleshanks: The Railway Cat' from *Old Possum's Book of Practical Cats*, written in 1935 for his godchildren. Skimbleshanks regularly travels on the Night Mail from Euston, which is a Sleeping Car Express, and the third stanza of the poem gives a wonderful description of the interior of a sleeping cabin, reminiscent of the ornate interiors of 1920s sleeper carriages.

Train companies were always keen to promote the more luxurious aspects of overnight travel, and nothing exemplifies this more clearly than the introduction of the Night Scotsman in the 1920s, a derivation of the famous Flying Scotsman train that ran daily between King's Cross and Edinburgh Waverley station. The 1920s and 1930s witnessed

Scottish Express Train at Euston Station *c.* 1909
Passengers boarding a LNWR express at Euston in around 1909. Note the smartly dressed member of staff, and the trolleys serving food and selling newspapers. (Science and Society Picture Library)

LNER sleeping car
No. 1157, 1930s.
(Science and Society
Picture Library)

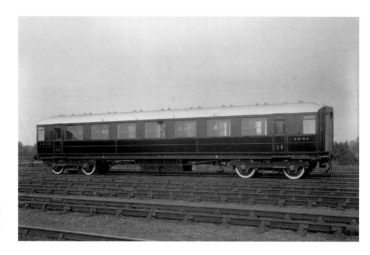

LNER Third Class
sleeping car No. 124,
from 1928–9, which
was used in ambulance
trains during the Second
World War. (Science and
Society Picture Library)

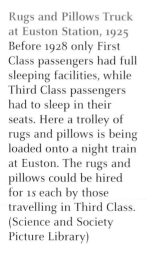

Rugs and Pillows Truck
at Euston Station, 1925
Before 1928 only First
Class passengers had full
sleeping facilities, while
Third Class passengers
had to sleep in their
seats. Here a trolley of
rugs and pillows is being
loaded onto a night train
at Euston. The rugs and
pillows could be hired
for 1s each by those
travelling in Third Class.
(Science and Society
Picture Library)

SLEEP O' NIGHTS

3RD CLASS SLEEPING CARS

ARE RUN ON THE UNDERNOTED TRAINS :---

SEPTEMBER 24th, 1928, until further notice.

From LONDON (Euston)				To LONDON (Euston)			
TO		p.m.		FROM		p.m.	
ABERDEEN	. . .	7 30	(Saturdays excepted)	ABERDEEN	. . .	7 50	(Weekdays)
INVERNESS	. . .	7 30	7.20 p.m. until October 12th inclusive. (Saturdays excepted) 7.20 p.m. until October 12th inclusive.	INVERNESS	. . .	4 0	(Weekdays) 4.55 p.m. until October 13th inclusive.
EDINBURGH (Princes St.)	.	11 5		EDINBURGH (Princes St.)	.	10 45	(Weekdays)
GLASGOW (Central)	. .	11 45		,,	,, . .	10 30	(Sundays)
STRANRAER	. . .	7 40	(Saturdays excepted)	GLASGOW (Central)	.	10 30	
,,	. . .	8 30	(Sundays)	STRANRAER	. . .	9 42	(Weekdays)
HOLYHEAD	. . .	8 45		HOLYHEAD	. . .	a.m. 12 13	

From LONDON (St. Pancras)				To LONDON (St. Pancras)			
TO		p.m.		FROM		p.m.	
				EDINBURGH (Waverley)	.	9 55	
EDINBURGH (Waverley)	.	9 15		GLASGOW (St. Enoch)	.	9 15	(Saturdays excepted)
GLASGOW (St. Enoch)	.	9 30	(Saturdays excepted)	,, (Central)		9 15	(Sundays)
,, (Central)	.	11 45	(Saturdays only)	,, (St. Enoch)	.	11 15	(Saturdays only)

The coaches will run daily, including Sundays, except as otherwise shown. Each coach will be divided into compartments, with four berths in each compartment (two upper and two lower), and each berth will be equipped with a pillow and rug.

The number of berths is strictly limited, and they will be allocated in order of application.

CHARGES AND RESERVATION OF BERTHS

A charge of 6s. between stations in England and Wales, and 7s. between stations in England and Scotland will be made, in addition to the Third Class fare, for the use of a berth.

Applications for the Reservation of berths should be made to the Station Master at Euston for the Down journey, and to the Station Master at the stations named above for the Up journey.

"Ladies only" compartments will be provided if asked for. Each compartment of four berths will be filled up before booking in the next. Preference for upper or lower berths will be granted as far as possible.

LMS LMS LMS LMS

Euston Station, London, N.W.1.   BEMROSE & SONS LTD. DERBY.   J. H. FOLLOWS. Vice-President.

Sleep O' Nights, 1928
A poster of 1928 advertising Third Class sleeping cars between London Euston and Aberdeen, Inverness, Edinburgh, Glasgow and Stranraer; and London St Pancras and Edinburgh or Glasgow. There was a charge of 7s for the berth in addition to the Third Class fare. (Science and Society Picture Library)

Interior of Third Class LNER sleeper, 1947, with interlocking compartments with alternate upper and lower berths, an ingenious attempt to fit more berths into a carriage. (Science and Society Picture Library)

Midland Sleeping Car No. 2778
Interior of Midland sleeping car No. 2778 showing the well upholstered berth with a receptacle for clothing, and a padded watch hook. There is a light switch and heating apparatus control above, and in the corner a fluted pedestal with wash basin. (Science and Society Picture Library)

the heyday of luxury train travel, and the 'Night Scotsman' was run in competition with the 'Night Scot' on the rival West Coast route. After the First World War the Night Scot departed Euston at 11.45 p.m., and arrived in Glasgow at 9.35 a.m. Two restaurant cars were added at Carlisle so that breakfast could be taken before arrival. On the way south the train ran non-stop between Glasgow and Crewe, a distance of 243.3 miles, pulled by a 4-6-0 Royal Scot, which was able to negotiate the summits of Beattock and Shap.

The train travelled on the route built by the Caledonian Railway in 1847, known originally as the Annandale route. The lines from Glasgow and Edinburgh converged at Carstairs Junction, still today the dividing point for the Lowland Sleeper. But there was another route between Edinburgh and Carlisle, which ran through Midlothian and the Borders. It was built by the North British Railway and was completed in 1862. This became known as the Waverley Route.

There is an atmospheric account of a journey over the Waverley Route between Edinburgh and Carlisle in September 1929, recorded in the pages of the *London and North Eastern Railway Magazine* of 1930 by R. A. H. Weight. He travelled on the footplate of Super-Pacific No. 2745, *Captain Cuttle*, which was pulling the 9.55 p.m. express to Carlisle and St Pancras, which included two LMS sleeping carriages, a First and Third, among the seventeen vehicles. The driver and fireman were father and son James and Thomas Kettle, who were both stationed at Carlisle at the Canal North British Shed.

He describes the departure from Edinburgh Waverley over the maze of tracks, through the tunnel and away through Niddrie South Junction inland on the long climb to Falahill Summit. Then *Captain Cuttle* coasted down to Galashiels, not running too fast so that the passengers could settle down to sleep as smoothly as possible. Then the engine was worked easily and with a full head of steam to Hawick and the final stretch into Carlisle. After negotiating the yards and junctions the train drew into the platform at Citadel station and pulled up at a signal from the platform inspector's lamp at precisely 12.30 a.m.

The writer left the train at Carlisle, and it continued its onward journey through the night to London St Pancras, but he had seen the power of Gresley's Pacifics on this testing route and the skill of the driver and fireman in handling these impressive locomotives. As a result of the Beeching Report this line was closed in 1969 because of dwindling traffic, but happily, part of the line has been re-opened as far as Tweedbank in 2015.

During the 1920s and 1930s wonderfully atmospheric posters were designed to advertise the glamour and safety of the night sleeper service. One advertising the Night Scotsman shows one of William Gresley's powerful A1 Pacific locomotives powering into the night, firebox blazing, carrying its sleeping passengers to Edinburgh and beyond. Such was its success that other named trains were introduced on both routes. The LNER introduced 'The Highlandman', which left London at 7.25 p.m. for Edinburgh with portions that split off for Fort William and Inverness. The Aberdonian left at 7.40 p.m. and a late evening train departed at 1.10 a.m., with carriages for Edinburgh, Glasgow, Aberdeen and Inverness.

Ewen Pinsent has fond memories of travelling on the Aberdonian in the 1930s to the family estate near Huntly:

I still recall going to the front of the Aberdonian before the great steam locomotive would appear out of the tunnel close to King's Cross to be yoked to the forward van.

Poster for the Night Scotsman This poster designed by Robert Bartlett in 1932 emphasises the speed of the train as it travels north towards Scotland by night. It was produced by the LNER to promote their overnight sleeper service, which left King's Cross at 10.25 p.m. (Science and Society Picture Library)

SCOTLAND BY "THE NIGHT SCOTSMAN"
KING'S CROSS — DEPART 10-25 P.M.
FIRST AND THIRD CLASS SLEEPERS

FIRST CLASS SLEEPING CAR

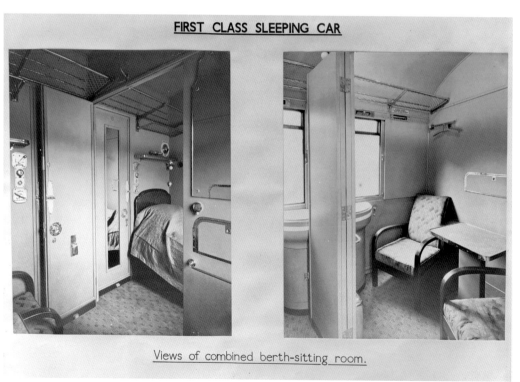

Views of combined berth-sitting room.

First Class LNER Sleeping Compartment 1930s
Combined berth and sitting room for VIPs in a First Class LNER sleeping carriage of the 1930s. The compartment was finished in Rexine wall coverings of cream and blue and included a shower compartment – a civilised but underused facility. (Science and Society Picture Library)

I think a Third Class berth cost 10/- and this continued during the war years. For that sum you got a berth in a four-berth compartment complete with a tartan rug and pillows, and an early morning tea tray. My father and mother would be in First Class single accommodation. I devoured chocolate digestive biscuits while my parents had dinner in the dining car.

Early in the morning the train would cross the Forth by the famous bridge, and the steel pillars could be 'heard' as the train traversed the Forth, a distinctive and unique sound. Later as a Naval Cadet at Eaton Hall in Cheshire I used to be taken to Crewe where the LMS sleeper train would carry me northwards.

The LMS introduced 'The Royal Highlander' in 1927, which served Aberdeen and Inverness. It left Euston at 7.30 p.m. in winter, reaching Perth at 5.24 a.m. where the Inverness and Aberdeen portions separated. This was from the beginning a 'dinner, bed and breakfast' train, which included three pairs of sleeping cars, both first and third, with composite carriages and brake vans. A restaurant car at the rear of the train was detached at Crewe, with another being attached at Perth to serve breakfast. At the height of summer three separate trains ran because of the demand. The train workings through the Highlands were usually handled by 4-6-0 Class 5 locomotives, based on William Stanier's Black Five – a successful mixed traffic steam engine, double-headed to cope with the steep gradients.

During the Second World War the route was an important artery taking military and naval traffic to and from bases at Invergordon and at Scapa Flow in the Orkney Islands. Two trains were required every evening in both directions: one leaving Euston at 7.20 p.m.

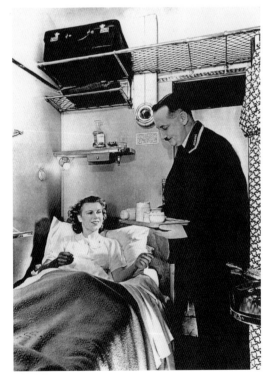

LNER First Class sleeping compartment on the Northern Belle. The attendant bears a remarkable resemblance to Peter Sellers! This was a 'luxury land cruise' pioneered by the LNER in the 1930s, consisting of First Class sleeping cars, restaurant cars and day carriages catering for sixty passengers with a staff of twenty-seven. (Science and Society Picture Library)

Corridor of 1930s LNER First Class sleeper. (Bedford Lemere Collection, Science and Society Picture Library)

for Inverness, and the second leaving at 7.30 p.m. for Perth. There is an evocative account of a journey by sleeper to the Orkney Islands in the period just before the Second World War in a novel called *The Story of the Man from Scapa Flow* (1940) by 'Taffrail', in which Captain John Stafford RN travels on the Aberdonian to Inverness before taking the slow train further north to Thurso:

> John liked sleepers. With their mahogany panelling, electric fans, tip-up wash basins, and other space-saving devices, they rather reminded him of cabins on board ship. Nevertheless, he rarely slept soundly. The rumbling of the wheels did not act as a soporific, and there was always the difficulty in the matter of ventilation ... but when he was called by the attendant at seven o'clock with a cup of tea and bread and butter, and the information that a breakfast car had been put on at Perth and would be taken off at Aviemore, the train was rushing through the delicious freshness of a wonderful spring morning like a rejuvenated giant.

During the war the LNER gained considerable kudos because a 1930s sleeping car of superior specification was rebuilt at the Doncaster Works for the private use of General

Left: Interior of LNER sleeping compartment. (Bedford Lemere Collection, Science and Society Picture Library)

Right: Interior of LNER sleeping compartment showing the shower. (Bedford Lemere Collection, Science and Society Picture Library)

Dwight D. Eisenhower as he toured military facilities around the country. Code-named 'Bayonet', it was armour-plated, with steel shutters for the windows. Inside it was fitted out with conference facilities and sleeping accommodation. Eisenhower was so delighted with it that he sent a personal letter of thanks to the LNER chairman. After the war ended the car was bought by the National Railroad Museum, Green Bay, Wisconsin, in 1968.

In the post-war years new sleeping cars continued to be built, including First and Third Class cars for the LNER with Thermotank pressure ventilation and steam heating. The first of the Third Class cars with two berths to all compartments entered service in April 1952. In 1948 the four major railway companies were nationalised to form British Railways (BR), ushering in a period that saw sweeping changes and a comprehensive programme of modernisation. This included the building of steel-bodied Mark 1 sleeping carriages between 1957 and 1964 to replace the fleets inherited from the LMS, LNER and GWR.

The standard Mark 1 BR coach was designed with a separate body and underframe and had a standard length of 64 ft 6 in. Melamine replaced wooden panelling, and the sleeping cars were fitted with two lavatories, eleven First Class berths and twenty-two Second Class, with some Composite carriages. Each carriage had a compartment for the attendant, and the interiors had a brighter and more functional look than pre-war stock. A total of 380 sleepers were built to service over thirty different sleeper routes then in operation.

In this post-war period, journey times by rail between London and Edinburgh were at least eight hours in length, domestic air services were in their infancy and the motorway

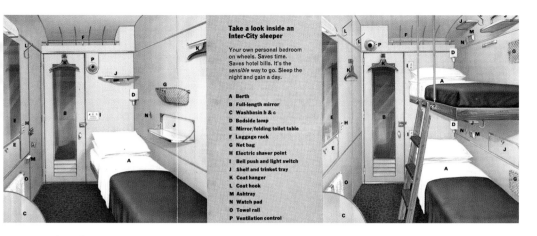

Mark 1 Sleeping Carriage: Interior of Cabin
The layout of a Mark 1 sleeper cabin depicted in a publicity brochure, showing both First and Second Class interiors. They were functional and practical, and the First Class berth cost 45s, while the Second Class twin berth supplement was 22s 6d per berth. (Author's Collection)

network did not exist, so overnight rail travel was a competitive and comfortable way to travel long distances.

My own experience of sleeper travel dates from 1959 when the Mark 1 carriages were in service – a great improvement on the older stock. The compartment included a rudimentary en suite facility by offering both a wash basin with hot and cold running water, and underneath it, on a hinged door, a chamber pot. When the pot was slotted into the door and pushed up, the contents were deposited directly onto the track. It was primitive and somewhat unhygienic, but it worked.

Sleeper booking fees were introduced in 1959 – 45s for First Class travel between England and Scotland, 22s 6d Second Class, and 14s for a four-berth cabin. This was because passengers often made reservations on more than one train as a form of insurance, with the result that some people failed to secure berths while trains left with empty berths. Booking fees were therefore added to the train fare, in the interests of fairness. In the mid-1960s the London–Edinburgh sleeper was advertised as providing 'interior-sprung mattresses, fresh linen, carpeted comfort, plenty of hot water, an electric razor point, morning tea and biscuits in bed, and the attendant only a bell push away'. Even better, an East Coast Route leaflet of 1963 boasted: 'The attendant has a limited supply of hot water bottles for those who like home comfort.'

In spite of strenuous marketing of the sleeper service, by this period competition from the car and the aeroplane had begun to cause a decline in the demand for sleeper travel and a number of the shorter-distance services were withdrawn, such as the Manchester–Plymouth and Paddington–Birkenhead trains. Other services, such as the King's Cross–Newcastle route, lasted longer, but by the late 1980s there were few passengers using them and they too were axed on economic grounds.

During the late 1960s and into the 1970s prospects for the overnight sleeper travel market were far from clear. The improved Inter-City brand and timings made daytime travel between London and the north practical and attractive. However, with the development of North Sea oil, overnight travel to Edinburgh, Dundee and Aberdeen

SLEEPING CAR EXPRESSES

FIRST AND SECOND CLASS SLEEPING ACCOMMODATION IS PROVIDED BY TRAINS RUNNING VIA THE "EAST COAST" ROUTE BETWEEN ENGLAND AND SCOTLAND AS UNDER:—

WEEK DAYS

[Detailed railway timetable showing departure and arrival times for named sleeping car expresses including "The Tynesider", "The Aberdonian", "The Night Scotsman", with stations such as London (King's Cross), Peterborough (North), Grantham, Newark (North Gate), Doncaster, York, Darlington, Ferryhill, Durham, Newcastle, Morpeth, Acklington, Alnmouth, Longhoughton, Berwick-upon-Tweed, Dunbar, Drem, Edinburgh (Waverley), Fort William, Dundee (Tay Bridge), Arbroath, Montrose, Aberdeen.]

WEEK DAYS

[Return timetable — Arrival times Tuesday to Sunday mornings inclusive]

SUNDAYS

[Sunday timetable.]

FOR CONTINUATION OF SUNDAY TRAINS AND NOTES, SEE PAGE 43

The East Coast BR timetable for 1959, showing details of the 'Sleeping Car Expresses', the Aberdonian departing King's Cross at 7.30 p.m. and the Night Scotsman, departing at 11.35 p.m. (Author's Collection)

remained popular. Perhaps because of this popularity, Dr Richard Beeching was (uncharacteristically) positive about sleeper travel in his 1963 report *The Reshaping of British Railways*. He concluded:

> On the Scottish routes, air makes quite serious inroads into the loading of day trains, and will continue to do so. On the other hand sleeper trains between London and Scotland continue to attract a satisfactory level of traffic, and there is good reason to suppose they can be improved and increased.
>
> Beeching HMSO 1963 p. 13

During the early 1970s BR was carrying about 900,000 sleeper passengers per year, so in spite of the competition from road and air, demand remained buoyant. During this period British Rail organised an annual publicity campaign, with a mobile information office that toured principal cities and towns in Scotland promoting Motorail and sleeper services. Local dignitaries, business people, travel agents and journalists were invited to a hotel, plied with whisky and shown two films, *Next Stop Scotland* and *Give Your Car a Holiday*, in the hope of publicising and promoting sleeper travel.

Guide to Principal Sleeper Services

6 May 1968 to 4 May 1969

LONDON—SCOTLAND
SCOTLAND—LONDON

Anglo-Scottish routes ————
Other routes ════════
British Transport Hotel near station ✱

For full details of all Sleeper Services in Britain including the new, faster West of England services, please enquire at your nearest British Rail Station, Travel Office or Appointed Travel Agent.

Above: Sleeper brochures advertising the service in the 1960s and '70s. (Author's Collection)

Right: Sleeper Services in the 1960s The map shows the sleeper services throughout the country, with the Anglo-Scottish routes picked out in bold. (Author's Collection)

On 2 April 1973, to celebrate 100 years of sleeper trains, a VIP centenary Night Scotsman ran from Glasgow via Edinburgh to London King's Cross, featuring a special dinner (melon cocktail, cold chicken, fruit flan and cheeseboard), and the passengers were presented with a commemorative brochure, toiletry case and a quarter bottle of champagne. There was an exhibition at Waverley station with replicas of two sleeping car compartments of 1873 and 1973, and a competition for 'Sleeper Beauties', who travelled on the train in period costumes and helped open the exhibition. In 1978 the British Railways Board launched a study about the future of sleeper travel, which concluded that if the carriages were upgraded there was still an important role for sleeper services on the long-haul routes. It was also clear that overall earnings per vehicle mile were about the same as a daytime vehicle, given the combination of the berth fee with a good proportion of full-fare passengers.

The option of upgrading the Mark 1 carriages was given serious consideration, but it was decided that it was impractical to match the standards that had been set by the Mark 2 coaches. The only viable way forward was to construct a brand new Mark 3 series of vehicles.

While the Mark 1 sleepers were regarded with affection by many who worked or travelled on them, they were, in the words of railway journalist Peter Kelly, 'noisy, claustrophobic, sometimes faintly smelly, and not easy to get to sleep in … but they were also homely in a certain kind of way' (*Rail Enthusiast*, July 1984). Kelly travelled on the last Mark 1 from Inverness to Glasgow on 14 May 1984 and described the rather gloomy interior decor of his berth, finished in turquoise blue and grey, with a large mirror on the opposite wall to the bed, various racks and shelves for clothes and personal belongings, purple and blue blankets and crisp white cotton sheets. Another feature was a window that would slide to let in fresh air, but a distinct disadvantage was the noisy ride, as you could hear every squeak and bang of the bogies. In the tiny galley at the end of the corridor, where the steward made all the early morning teas and coffees, conditions were cramped and often dirty, but nevertheless the attendants managed to provide a civilized service for their passengers.

There were four variants of the Mark 1 Sleeper: Sleeping Car First, Sleeping Car Composite, Sleeping Car Second and Sleeping Car Convertible. Over time, and increasingly from 1979 onwards, numbers were withdrawn and stored in Tinsley Yard, Sheffield, prior to scrapping. As they contained asbestos insulation they were disposed of at Berry's of Leicester and Mayer Newman at Snailwell near Newmarket.

Then, disastrously, in July 1978 there was a tragic accident involving a sleeping car at Taunton, when bed linen stacked by a heater on the Paddington–Penzance sleeper caught fire, killing twelve passengers. The subsequent inquiry called for major changes to sleeper accommodation, including the use of non-flammable materials, refined fire alarm systems and the introduction of smoke detectors. These modifications resulted in an overspend on the Mark 3 project and a delay of nine months.

In fact, as early as 1973 David Bowick, BR Chief Executive (Railways), had proposed the construction of a new generation of sleeping cars based on the revenue-earning potential of sleeper trains and the idea of marketing them as travelling hotels with improved standards and enhanced refreshment facilities. In 1975 the rolling stock design engineer, H. Wilcock, proposed that toilet facilities should be incorporated into each compartment because he was confident that the problems associated with the collection and storage of effluent could be overcome. He added: 'If these facilities are not provided I am convinced that their absence would encourage much less hygienic practices on the part of at least a proportion of sleeping car passengers.'

Short-sightedly, when the order for 236 new Mark 3 coaches was submitted in August 1979, chamber pots disappeared from the cabins, but only two toilets at the end of each carriage replaced them. The BR Board did not take into account the fact that the public were demanding higher standards, and were beginning to expect en suite facilities in hotel bedrooms.

Those who used the service regularly in the 1980s regretted the removal of the potty on health and safety grounds, and the then Permanent Secretary of State at the Scottish Office, later Chancellor of Glasgow University, Sir William Fraser GCB was moved to compose the following poem:

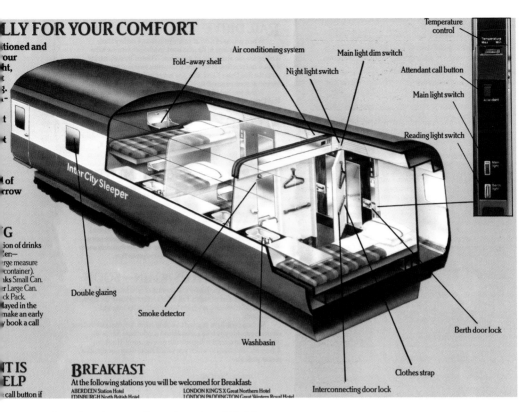

Temperature control

Air conditioning system

Main light dim switch

Fold-away shelf

Night light switch

Attendant call button

Main light switch

Reading light switch

InterCity Sleeper

Double glazing

Smoke detector

Berth door lock

Washbasin

Clothes strap

BREAKFAST
At the following stations you will be welcomed for Breakfast:
ABERDEEN Station Hotel   LONDON KING'S X Great Northern Hotel
EDINBURGH North British Hotel   LONDON PADDINGTON Great Western Royal Hotel

Interconnecting door lock

Mark 3 Sleeping Carriage: Interior of Cabin

This cut-away diagram shows the remodelled Mark 3 cabin, with a more sophisticated air-conditioning system, smoke detector and double-glazed windows. The brochure described the facilities available, and added: 'For everyone's comfort it would be appreciated if smokers will refrain from smoking in the sleeping compartments.' (Science and Society Picture Library)

THE MARK THREE SLEEPER

Maist every Monday evenin' I gae headin' south by train,
And early Friday mornin' I'm at Waverley again.
Aye, I'm thirled tae the sleepers – but of late there's been a change:
The brand new travellin' bedroom is tae me a wee thing strange.
Noo its all hygenic plastic – but they've made an awfu' botch.
For it hisna got a potty or a place to hang your watch.

I dinna like the Shuttle: they treat ye a' like sheep:
I canna use the buses though I'm told they're fine and cheap.
I much prefer tae spend the night relaxin' in a train:
Ye snib the door, an there ye are, just quietly on yer ain,
Or gaithered wi a frien' or twa tae hae a wee debauch,
And yet – there's no a potty or a place to hang your watch.

43

In yon auld, shoogly sleepers I've been bobbin like a cork.
I could tell the bridge at Selby or the points just north of York,
I could hear yon noisy rattle on the bridge across the Tyne.
But noo ... the sole disturbance is the air-conditioner's whine.
Ye still get Schweppe's water tae dilute your glass of Scotch,
But ye dinna get a potty or a place to hang your watch.

Sir William's lament was echoed by many, but the die was already cast. A perception that the sleeper facilities were lagging behind the times, coupled with the economic recession of the early 1980s, were significant reasons why the sleeping car market began to decline during this period.

Nevertheless, the Mark 3 carriages began to be delivered from BR's Derby Works in November 1981. There were 146 cars that comprised twelve berths and a pantry, and ninety cars that comprised thirteen berths with no pantry – unlike the Mark 1 stock, no differentiation was made between First and Second Class vehicles; instead, in First Class cabins the upper berth was simply folded away. The cost of the fleet renewal was £60 million. Passengers were charged either a First Class fare plus a £15 berth fee for single occupancy, or a Second Class fare plus an £11 berth fee for double occupancy. The cars could thus be used more flexibly according to demand. From May 1984 inclusive sleeper prices were advertised to cover both the rail fare and the berth fee, doing away with the off-putting 'sleeper supplement'.

Publicity brochures of the 1980s showed a cut-away diagram of the carriage, and included pictures of a smartly uniformed attendant looking after both businessmen and families. Slogans such as 'In Quiet Comfort on new Inter-City Sleepers', 'Welcome aboard your travelling hotel', 'Sleep the night and gain a day', and 'The Journey of a Night Time' promoted the benefits of the sophisticated experience of travelling in the new Mark 3 sleepers.

The publicity leaflets also emphasised the comfort, security and safety of the modern carriages, and reflected the social changes of the period. Sleepers were no longer the exclusive preserve of grouse-shooting gentry, but were increasingly being used by a much wider cross-section of the population. By the end of 1983 most of the Mark 1 vehicles had been withdrawn and sent to the scrapyard. Because the Mark 3 carriages were electrically heated, a second engine was fitted behind the main locomotive to act as a mobile generator. They were called ETHELS (Electric Train Heat Ex Locomotives). They provided the power to work the lighting, heating and air-conditioning in the sleeper carriages, until Class 37 locomotives were fitted with ETH equipment. Because of the air-braking system and retention lavatories fitted in the Mark 3s, the new stock had to work in complete formations, which meant reshaping the operation into eight sets covering four nightly workings in each direction. The trains were hauled by Class 47 locomotives pulling a weight of 455 tonnes.

In spite of the introduction of this new fleet of coaches, with their superior comfort and smoother ride, their numbers began to be reduced almost immediately because of changes in the market for long-distance travel. I have already mentioned the increased competition from road and air. On the railways the main issue was the vast improvement in journey times between major cities on the East and West Coast Main Lines. Passengers could now travel by train and return home to their own beds in a day. The revenue from the sleepers bore no comparison with day travel, and needed substantial subsidy.

Left: BR poster advertising the new Mark 3 sleepers, and the routes between Bristol, Edinburgh and Glasgow. (Science and Society Picture Library)

Right: Inter-City Sleepers
A BR poster and leaflet of 1985 advertising Saver Fares, produced for BR Central Advertising Services, promoting sleeper services between London, Bristol or Birmingham and Scotland. (Science and Society Picture Library)

The 1980s was therefore a difficult period for the sleepers, and standards unfortunately slipped. Three stories illustrate the point. Sarah Bromage recalls getting into her bunk just outside Glasgow on the journey south to find cockroaches running around in her bed. When she went to look for an attendant she found the carriage doors locked, and in desperation pulled the communication cord. The train juddered to a halt and train officials climbed in. The cockroach story didn't impress them, but she was moved to another compartment. When she wrote to complain, she received an amusing letter telling her that she didn't deserve compensation as she had probably had a lot of fun pulling the cord!

During the same period a senior civil servant in the Scottish Office was travelling home to Edinburgh from London when he discovered fleas in his cabin. Back in his office he fired off a strong complaint to the sleeper authorities. In due course he received a reply personally offering profuse apologies and a recital of all the steps that were taken each day to ensure the utmost cleanliness. Somewhat mollified, he was on the point of putting the letter to one side when he noticed another piece of paper in the envelope. This turned out to be a manuscript note, which said: 'Send him the Bug Letter, Charlie.'

Worse still, Clive Robinson, travelling from King's Cross to Edinburgh in about 1980, remembers sharing his two-berth cabin with a man who entered the compartment having only just caught the train, and who promptly lit a cigarette. In the wake of the 1978 Taunton fire this was strictly against the rules, but Clive saw he was relieved to have caught the train, and in any case recognised him as a well-known Scottish journalist. A second cigarette was lit with the comment that he wasn't a chain smoker. When a third was produced, and he showed no sign of settling down for the night, Clive felt obliged to protest and he grumpily obliged by putting it out. Fortunately he was up early the next morning and out of the carriage before any further anti-social activity was possible. But in the days before the smoking ban, such behaviour was just one more disincentive to travelling in confined spaces.

Responding to the pressures facing sleeper travel, Dr John Prideaux, Director of BR Inter-City, reorganised the sleeper services in 1988, withdrawing sleepers from the East Coast Main Line and concentrating Anglo-Scottish services on Euston and the West Coast Main Line. From then onwards, just two services operated each night, consisting of sixteen-car trains, the first running to Aberdeen, Inverness and Fort William, dividing at Edinburgh, and the second later train to Glasgow and Edinburgh, dividing at Carstairs. The popular lounge cars were introduced, serving simple cooked meals, light refreshments and drinks. The number of intermediate stops was reduced and speeds were limited to 80 mph, giving a smoother ride. This rationalisation meant that far fewer vehicles were needed. Those surplus to requirements were either stored, sent for scrap, used for luxury land cruise stock, or given a new lease of life as staff dormitory vehicles, and on heritage railways. The sleeper fleet was part of the Inter-City brand, delivering an income of around £25 million, or 3.5 per cent of the total Inter-City income. In spite of this the service continued to be trimmed, and in May 1990 the London–Stranraer sleeper, known as 'The Paddy', was withdrawn. This train featured in a 1930s detective story by Freeman Wills Crofts, *Inspector French and Sir John Magill's Last Journey*. The plot revolves around

Inter-City brochures advertising the Royal Highlander, the West Highlander and the Night Scotsman from the 1980s. (Author's Collection)

a murder on the Euston–Stranraer boat train, which takes place in interconnecting sleeper compartments and displays the author's detailed knowledge of the working of the railways.

Sadly, by the end of the twentieth century the passenger numbers on this romantic train had declined to such an extent (an average of ten people per week day) that the service had become uneconomical. Every time this happened to specific sleeper trains there was a predictable outcry from local MPs and others, but Inter-City worked to a commercial remit and needed to balance its books.

When the railways were privatised in the 1990s the government wanted the sleeper services to be financially viable or to be scrapped. The government therefore intended to axe the subsidies to British Rail, which would have meant the closure of the Fort William Sleeper and Motorail. ScotRail, who were just about to take over the Sleeper operation, maintained that they could not continue the Fort William service without a £3 million subsidy, claiming that the subsidy per passenger was £450, although independent experts put it at less than £50 per passenger.

Campaign groups were formed, including 'The London Friends of the West Highland Lines', and protests were held at Fort William. The campaign was masterminded by Hugh Raven, who has a family estate in the north-west of Scotland, but who lived in Kensington. Peter Brown was the Secretary and John Savery was Treasurer. Ian Tegner, who was also involved in the campaign, takes up the story:

> As we dug deeper into the available information we realised how very devious were the statistics and public interest propaganda, and the extent to which Government was sheltering behind the new office of Rail Regulator and vice versa. As we formed relationships with honest senior rail executives, we recognised their informed frustration with the political farce. There appeared to be no coherent transport policy – the position of the railways being viewed in a vacuum with no consideration of the broader economic impact, and with a shambolic costing system which was then blatantly cooked to achieve a pre-determined case for closure. In the midst of the consultation period the Rail Regulator Roger Salmon announced without warning that the subsidy would be cancelled, and British Rail stated that the service would cease to operate on 28th May 1995 just at the beginning of the tourist season. We had hoped that our campaign would result in a resort to reason, but we had failed to reckon with the bureaucrats' ignorance of the concept of rationality.
>
> We submitted our response to the "consultation" in July 1995. Our closely argued case was accompanied by a petition against closure signed by over 20,000 people.
>
> A court ruling by Lord Kirkwood, upheld on appeal, confirmed that British Rail could not legally close a section of line which was used only to take the sleeper trains round Glasgow, and that their alternative proposal to run ghost trains was not acceptable. Notwithstanding this case, British Rail withdrew the sleeper service from their advertised timetables and for a time it became almost impossible to book a ticket on it, even though it continued to run. In the end we won the battle and lost the war. The legal ruling ensured that the service continued to operate, but the case for expansion and exploitation made by us was buried.

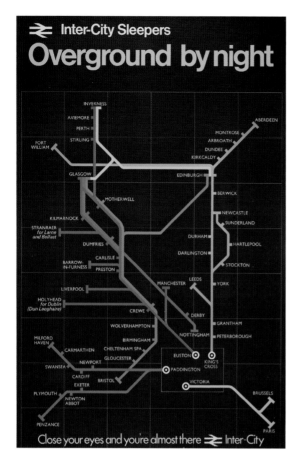

Inter-City Sleeper network in the 1980s. (Science and Society Picture Library)

The Fort William service was nevertheless given a reprieve, thanks largely to the campaign, and it was relaunched by ScotRail as part of the Caledonian Sleeper.

In fact, the Scottish sleeper was the final BR passenger service to run before the privatisation of the railways on 31 March 1997. Just before midnight the Up Sleeper left Edinburgh Waverley for Euston, waved off by the BR Chairman and Chief Executive John Welsby, five minutes before contracts were signed transferring ScotRail to private ownership with National Express Group. After nearly fifty years as part of a nationalised railway, the sleepers were being run by a multinational public transport company which operated bus, coach and train services in the UK and elsewhere. It was an historic moment, marked by the distribution on the train of a special commemorative whisky miniature, but apart from that the passengers didn't seem to care about the change of ownership. If they registered any reaction at all they probably hoped for a better service with better facilities. Under the privatised ScotRail individual trains were branded as The Night Caledonian (to Glasgow), Night Scotsman (to Edinburgh), Night Aberdonian, Royal Highlander (to Inverness) and the West Highlander (to Fort William). As already noted, from this period only two trains ran out of Euston, the Highland Sleeper and the Lowland Sleeper. The two services are formed of two eight-car sections joined together to form a sixteen-car formation for the first part of the journey. This makes the Caledonian Sleeper the longest, and the heaviest, passenger train in Britain.

As part of its franchise ScotRail undertook a programme of refurbishment and the cabin interiors were fitted with new blinds, wash basins and worktops, and furnished in two-tone blue with off-white hard surfaces. First Class passengers were given a pack of toiletries, with a simpler pack for Standard Class. First Class breakfast trays offered yoghurt, orange juice, a bacon roll and china cups, plates and saucers, with fresh tea or coffee. The lounge cars were refurbished, and offered a wider menu of microwaved food, snacks and drinks. Staffing levels were, and remain, high, with a cabin attendant for every two carriages, a lounge car steward and a train manager.

From the earliest days of the railways, staff had worn uniforms for ease of identification and to emphasise their authority and status as railway employees. Grades of staff who were in constant contact with the public were given extra smart uniforms of a semi-military kind, with ornate buttons and gold braid, and a cap with a badge. When BR developed its corporate image in the 1960s the uniform moved away from the traditional navy blue, and in the franchise era the uniforms reflect the styles and colour schemes of the different train operating companies, with a less militaristic look.

On the sleepers the instructions given to attendants emphasised the importance of the uniform, insisting that it be worn at all times. An Inter-City leaflet proclaimed, 'You are the company's frontline ambassador,' and stated that shirts or blouses were to be laundered every night. 'Nail varnish is not permitted, and necklaces and bracelets are not to be worn.' Staff had to check in at least half an hour before boarding time, check their equipment and be in position by the platform door to give a friendly welcome, examine tickets and ask what time passengers wanted a morning call. There was always a great emphasis on safety, and earlier instructions included, 'Stewards must remain vigilant at all times,' and 'Stewards must frequently patrol the corridors,' to keep good order and maintain security.

The sleeping car attendants often notice things that the casual traveller would miss. A few years ago an attendant observed that a couple of unconventional-looking passengers were using the Inverness sleeper quite frequently. He noticed that although they were booked through to Inverness, they often got off earlier, frequently at Aviemore. After a while his suspicions were aroused to the extent that he notified the police, and the next time they got off the train the police were waiting for them. It turned out that they were couriers for a drug gang based in the Midlands, and as a result the gang was caught and jailed.

No. 92014 at Euston having hauled the Highland Sleeper from Edinburgh on Friday 4 August 2017. (Stuart Vallis)

A range of helpful and informative leaflets were provided in the cabins for passengers, telling them about the refreshments available and information about what to do on arrival at London, Inverness or Fort William. The food served in the lounge car hardly compared with the full restaurant car service of previous decades, but offered a range of hot snacks and a wide variety of malt whiskies. Under ScotRail's tenure the food began to improve, with a 'Dinner Menu' consisting of three courses and offering salmon, chicken korma or beef casserole.

In January 2000 sitting carriages were introduced, with eleven Mark 2 carriages being refurbished with First Class reclining seats, and the Mark 3 sleeping carriages were refurbished in a purple and blue livery.

When ScotRail took over the service they decided to base most vehicle maintenance work at Inverness, where there was spare capacity and a skilled workforce. Maintenance was worked on an 8 x 8 x 8 basis, i.e. eight vehicle sets visiting their home depot every eight days. There are also service facilities at Aberdeen, Polmadie, Fort William and Wembley. Catering and laundry services are organised to keep the trains fully stocked and cleaning is contracted out at all the locations except Fort William.

In 2011, looking ahead to the renewal of the ScotRail franchise in 2015, Transport-Scotland held a consultation about rail services, which included a section on the Caledonian Sleeper. During 2010–11 passenger numbers on the sleepers were 274,000 – an increase of 31 per cent over the previous five years. It was estimated that Scottish sleepers cost £21 million per year, or around £175 per passenger, excluding track access charges. The service called at thirty-six stations in Scotland.

Over 1,200 responses were received from the consultation process, both from organisations and individuals, which revealed a strong desire for the service to continue, although opinion was divided about whether the service should be contracted separately or be part of the ScotRail franchise. It was felt to be a vital link for both business and tourism, a viable alternative to air travel, and an important asset for the economy of the Highlands. The consultation also revealed a desire for better on-board facilities, such as en suite toilets and showers, and WiFi provision, and there was a call for better marketing, and improved booking arrangements. Some respondents also favoured Oban as an additional destination, with better bus connectivity between Oban and Fort William.

At the time of the consultation the Scottish government agreed to match a £50 million offer from the Chancellor of the Exchequer to fund new carriages and improved facilities.

As a result of the consultation and the bidding process the Scottish government announced in 2012 that from April 2015 the Caledonian Sleeper would be operated under a separate franchise which had been awarded to Serco, the outsourcing conglomerate whose 100,000 employees also operate the Trident nuclear submarine base on the Clyde, the Yarl's Wood Immigration Centre in Bedfordshire, and prisons, call centres and schools across the country on behalf of its customers. It also operates the NorthLink Ferries that connect the Orkney and Shetland Islands with the mainland of Scotland.

The Caledonian Sleeper became Britain's newest (2015) franchise, in order to meet Transport Scotland's desire to transform the Sleeper service into a better quality 'hotel-type' experience that would promote night time travel between Scotland and England. The managing director, Peter Strachan, spoke of his desire to transform all aspects of the sleeper operation, including marketing, sales, on-train hospitality, station facilities for sleeper passengers, and vehicle maintenance. He has made immediate changes since April

2015, including reliveried trains, with branding designed by Weber Shandwick, a revamped website with online booking, the ability to make bookings up to twelve months in advance, and improved catering, with enhanced menus in the lounge car, food and drink sourced from north of the border, attendants dressed in new Harris tweed and tartan uniforms, and a sleepover kit from Arran Aromatics, all produced in Scotland. But the real game-changer is the commissioning of seventy-five new sleeper coaches from CAF in Spain, which are being introduced into service in April 2018. The fleet of Mark 2 and 3 carriages is the oldest fleet of any train operating company, averaging thirty-eight years of age, and they have been feeling and looking tired. They are being retired from service as the new fleet of Mark 5 carriages comes into operation. British train builders lost out to CAF (Construcciones y Auxiliar de Ferrocarriles), a Spanish train maker based in Beasain. The new coaches will be maintained by Alstom at their Polmadie (Glasgow) and Wembley (London) traincare centres with daily servicing being carried out at Aberdeen, Fort William and Inverness. The fleet is composed of eleven seated coaches, ten 'club cars', fourteen PRM-TSI (Persons with Reduced Mobility-Technical Specification for Interoperability) compliant sleeper vehicles, and forty sleeper coaches.

The new Mark 5 carriages offer four ways to travel overnight: Cradle Seats, Pod Flatbeds, Berths and En Suite Berths. The Cradle Seats recline and have footrests, while the Pod Flatbeds fully recline from a seat into a bed and offer a privacy screen and a reading light. The berths are an upgraded version of the existing ones, with a new internal decor by designer Ian Smith and upgraded panels for phone charging and WiFi. There are also berths that are fully compliant with the Disability Discrimination Act. The En Suite Berths provide dedicated toilet and shower facilities, and there is the option of double-bed accommodation – a first for overnight travel in the UK. There is also a new key-card entry system to ensure ease of access combined with security. The lounge car design has been upgraded with more seating options for maximum flexibility. All these improvements

The new Caledonian Sleeper logo. (Stuart Vallis)

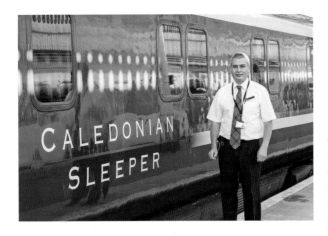

The old carriage branding of the Caledonian Sleeper, with Cesar, the attendant, dressed in the new uniform on the platform at Aberdeen, Wednesday 2 August 2017. (Stuart Vallis)

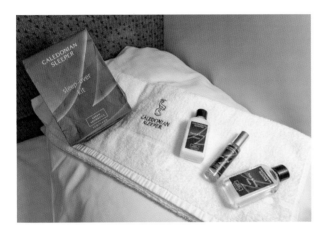

Compartment interior showing a selection of toiletries from the sleep-over kit designed by Arran Aromatics of Scotland. (Stuart Vallis)

create a more hotel-style experience rather than the previous more utilitarian approach, a return to the days of luxury travel epitomised by the Night Scotsman of the 1920s and 1930s. The company has moved the operating headquarters to Inverness, and the staff who came over from ScotRail have received new training and have been encouraged to engage fully with the new company and embrace these innovations.

Locomotives and crews are provided by GB Railfreight, although in recent years there have been problems with the engines. Class 92 locomotives were introduced to pull the sleepers, but after a series of failures they were taken off and replaced with Class 90s hired from Freightliner while modifications were made to the Class 92s. The 92s were originally planned as Channel Tunnel locomotives and were fitted with duplicate systems, so that if one converter failed the other would still deliver sufficient power to allow the train to reach its destination. However, having been stored in the open for a number of years, this exposure, together with sensitive electronics, caused reliability problems when they were returned to service. They have now settled down and are performing reliably on the West Coast Main Line.

GBRF also experienced problems with the Class 73 locomotives that were being used to haul the portions of the Highland Sleeper north of Edinburgh to Aberdeen, Fort William and Inverness. They have had to put on a pair of the locomotives, with Class 66s being run in tandem on each of the trains because the 73s cannot be run on full power for technical reasons. This ensures that the trains keep to time, but has not prevented occasional failures. Work has been undertaken to modify the Class 92 locomotives, and both the 73s and the 92s require modifications to fit Dellner couplers compatible with the Mark 5 carriages. Meanwhile, as the majority of GBRF drivers had not driven passenger trains before because they were used to working on freight services, they were given training to drive somewhat more gently to avoid any 'snatching' as the locomotives leave the stations, and slow down before pulling into the platform. When you travel on the overnight sleepers you are usually unaware of the sheer complexity of the sleeper operation. There are effectively seven arrivals every day into stations in Scotland and London, and each has its own engine and driver, who may only take the train on part of its journey before another driver takes over. The schedules allow generous amounts of spare running time, but the sleepers have to maintain their schedules, fit in with overnight freight trains and in the morning are competing with commuter trains, which often take preference if the sleeper is running late. The early hours stop at Carlisle is provided so that the shunter responsible for splitting the Lowland Sleeper at Carstairs can come on board, and at the end of their journeys the empty stock has to be taken away for cleaning and maintenance and brought back for the next night's run. John Heaton, in an article in *The Railway Magazine* for June 2017, gives an excellent account of travelling with the driver in the cab of a Class 92 on the London to Glasgow sleeper that highlights the logistical complexities involved, of which the sleeping passengers will be blissfully unaware.

At the time of writing there is talk of the possibility of transferring sleeper operations to King's Cross or even St Pancras because of the rebuilding of Euston as part of HS2. The environment at Euston is not very attractive as the departure point for the upgraded service, and both King's Cross and St Pancras are much more elegant settings for experiencing the new sleeper service. There has also been talk of a new 'internal' Scottish sleeper service operating between Thurso in the far north and Glasgow/Edinburgh, connecting with the Stromness–Scrabster ferries and travelling via Aberdeen. The plan is to use Mark 3 vehicles that will be made redundant with the arrival of the new carriages. These are ideas for the future, but they show that with the new franchise there is renewed interest in a night sleeper service, and renewed energy on the part of both government and operator to make Caledonian Sleeper an iconic brand and a flagship for Scottish business and tourist trade expansion. Serco is also keen to encourage the shooting fraternity to keep using the sleeper. In spite of a ban on firearms on ScotRail trains, Serco CEO Rupert Soames has announced that the Caledonian Sleeper welcomes 'responsible customers with licensed firearms', which is timely news in view of the fact that field sports tourism injects £155 million a year into the Scottish economy.

No longer is a modern sleeper merely a converted railway carriage, but a purpose-designed unit, with all the services built-in and close at hand. It is a genuine 'hotel on wheels'.

At the time of the Fort William sleeper battle in 1995 a campaigner commented, 'You know, the sleeper service could be the UK's equivalent of the Orient Express,' and this new development of the service under Serco means that that aspiration is becoming a reality. Stylish, tasteful, and comfortable, passengers can now enjoy an experience that echoes the pre-war glory days of Anglo-Scottish night-time travel. It is certainly a lot better than two poles, some webbing and a cushion!

3

'Make the Going Eazzzzzzzy...': The Motorail Era

Being able to take your personal vehicle with you on a train journey was something that really came into its own in the era of mass car ownership, but there were historical precedents stretching back almost to the beginning of the railways. A lithograph of 1830 from a painting by Charles Vignoles is entitled 'View of a Train of Carriages Drawn by a Locomotive Steam Engine on a Railway'. It shows the locomotive *Novelty* pulling four trucks, two of which carry private carriages, one open and the other closed.

Later on, *Bradshaw's Guide* for 1875 gives details of the LNER 8.10 a.m. service to Scotland from King's Cross, and states, 'Horse and Carriage Train will run only when necessary.' The equivalent service from Euston on the Midland Main Line departs at 9.30 a.m., 'for Horses and Private Carriages only'. In the early twentieth century an LNER poster of 1935 advertises: 'Take your car by LNER.' But the real challenge came in the post-war period.

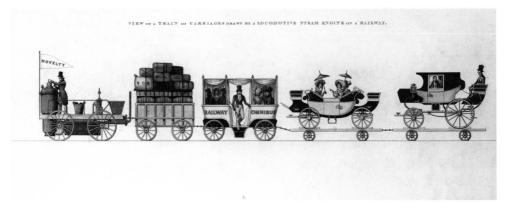

Carriages Conveyed by Railway Wagon, c. 1830.
This early lithograph from a painting by Charles Vignoles shows the locomotive *Novelty* pulling four carriages, including two wagons that convey private carriages – the precursor of the Motorail era. (Science and Society Picture Library)

Above: An open carriage truck waits at the dock at Strathcarron station on the line to Kyle of Lochalsh in 1910, loaded with a Wolseley-Siddeley motor car owned by Lieutenant Mark Sprot of the Scots Greys cavalry barracks, Norwich, and Riddell Estate, Lilliesleaf. The locomotive, HR No. 88, is heading an Up train. (Highland Railway Society Collection)

Right: Poster Advertising Car Transporter 1935
'Take Your Car by LNER', advertising rates of 3*d* per mile for a single journey, and 1½*d* per mile for the return journey. (Artwork by Frank Newbold)

From the 1960s onwards British Rail's main rival was rapidly increasing car ownership and the expansion of the motorway network. BR's strategy was to try to work with the nation's desire for car ownership, and they came up with the idea of taking your car with you on your train journey, which was something the airlines simply couldn't copy.

This service started in the summer of 1955, when the motorway network did not yet exist and the average family car was slower and less powerful than it later became. So for those travelling to Scotland it made great sense to spend the night on board the train rather than finding a hotel for an overnight stop. After all, the journey from London King's Cross to Perth was 830 miles – a formidable undertaking that by car would occupy the best part of four days travel for the return trip. Thus was born the Anglo-Scottish Car Carrier, which became Motorail in 1966.

A publicity brochure of 1961 proclaimed:

Like thousands of other carefree motorists begin your holiday at a railway station. Make for the open road – by train. Climb into your sleeping berth and arrive fresh as a daisy to pick up your car at your destination the next morning.

There are three kinds of car-carrying services operated by British Railways – with the CAR-SLEEPER and CAR-CARRIER service passenger and car travel by the same

---

THE CAR-SLEEPER LIMITED
LONDON (King's Cross) — PERTH

SECOND CLASS ONLY

EVERY NIGHT EXCEPT FRIDAYS

		Weekdays	Sundays
		pm	pm
London (King's Cross) .. .. ..dep 8 5	Perth .. ..dep 8 0	7 40	
am		am	am
Perth .. ..arr 5A40	London (King's Cross).arr 6 15	6 15	

A Passengers may remain in Sleeping Berths until 6 30 am

RETURN FARES
(inclusive of conveyance of car in covered
van, seating and sleeping accommodation)

	£ s. d.
Driver and car	18 10 0
Each additional adult passenger accompanying	6 0 0
Children age 3 and under 14	3 15 0

BOOKING ARRANGEMENTS

As accommodation is limited, bookings should be made in advance and these will be confirmed by receipt of remittance, which, in any case, must be made not less than 28 days before the date of travel. Tickets and travel information will be issued a few days before passengers travel.

Accommodation will be reserved ONLY for holders of the special tickets specifying the train and date of travel. By arrangement packed suppers can be provided, and breakfasts served on arrival at either Perth or London.

Further information may be had on application to the Traffic Manager, Car Sleeper Office, British Railways (Eastern Region), King's Cross station, London, N.I. or at any British Railways station, town office or ticket agent.

Dogs—A limited number of dogs accompanying passengers travelling by the CAR-SLEEPER will be conveyed in the Guard's van. Rates will be quoted upon request. Dogs are NOT permitted to travel in sleeping cars, nor in the motor cars.

The Car Sleeper Limited
This 1959 advertisement for the Car Sleeper from King's Cross to Perth shows a departure time from King's Cross of 8.05 p.m., arriving at Perth at 5.40 a.m. The return fare for driver and car was £18 10s 0s, with each additional adult paying £6 0s 0d, and children £3 15s 0d. Notice that dogs were not allowed in the sleeping berths. (Author's Collection)

Motorail Terminal, 1967
Cars being loaded into covered wagons at the Caledonian Road loading bay in London in 1967. Note the sparse facilities and the white-coated attendant. (Science and Society Picture Library)

train. With the CAR-TOURIST service passenger and car travel by separate trains, the car through the night and the passenger by day or night.

At first passenger accommodation was provided in the old four-berth Third Class sleeping cars, later replaced by the BR Mark 1 vehicles, and the cars were conveyed in ten four-wheeled vans. The cars were loaded at the King's Cross Horse/Motor Loading Bay, and each train carried twenty cars. The train left at 7.45 p.m., with packed suppers provided, reaching Perth at 5.30 a.m., where passengers could remain on board or move to the station refreshment room for breakfast while the cars were unloaded. The service proved an instant success and the frequency was increased to five nights a week. This is the service I remember so well because after holidays using the Royal Highlander, my parents – now owning a smart new Morris Oxford – transferred thereafter to the car-carrier, which we used frequently during the 1960s.

In 1957 the LMS introduced a Marylebone–Glasgow service, and in 1958 a Sutton Coldfield–Sterling service, thereby linking the Midlands with Scotland. A Glasgow–Eastbourne service was introduced in 1961. A winter time service between King's Cross and Edinburgh began in 1956 and was soon extended to Aberdeen, Perth and Inverness, running every night of the week.

Gerald Moule remembers a journey in the early 1960s from Euston to Sterling, when travelling as a fifteen-year-old boy with his parents. They had already noticed that the sleeper was filled with shooting parties, as it was around the time of the 'Glorious Twelfth', and had

observed many guns and related equipment being loaded onto the train. On entering the restaurant car, which served as a bar, there in the middle was Prime Minister Harold Macmillan holding court with several shooting friends. After the family had enjoyed a nightcap they returned to their bunks, leaving the PM's party, which looked all set to carry on into the early hours while the train thundered northwards, pulled by a Coronation Class locomotive.

The London departure point was moved in 1960 to the former Caledonian Road Cattle Station at Holloway Road, and new double-decker covered vans were introduced in 1962, each carrying six cars. The charge was £15 return for car and driver, with special rates for additional passengers.

By now all overnight trains were formed of Mark 1 sleepers with full bedding. The Mark 1 carriage, built between 1957 and 1964, was a considerable improvement on previous coaches built of wood, but still did not have an integrated structure, i.e. the body was separate from the underframe. Toilets flushed directly onto the track, and windows in the compartments could be opened by hand. This was a blessing in hot weather as the heating/air-conditioning system was primitive. It also meant that when we trundled over the Forth

The Motorail terminal at Kensington Olympia. (Science and Society Picture Library)

Motorail staff offloading cars. (Science and Society Picture Library)

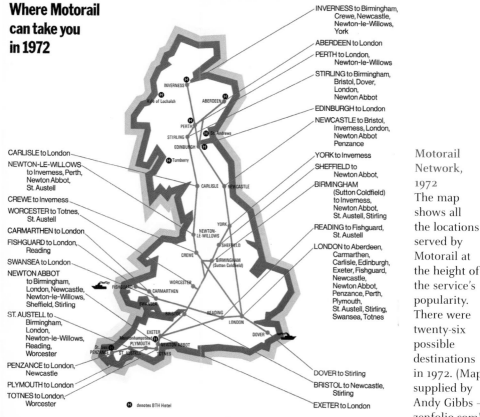

Where Motorail can take you in 1972

INVERNESS to Birmingham, Crewe, Newcastle, Newton-le-Willows, York

ABERDEEN to London

PERTH to London, Newton-le-Willows

STIRLING to Birmingham, Bristol, Dover, London, Newton Abbot

EDINBURGH to London

NEWCASTLE to Bristol, Inverness, London, Newton Abbot, Penzance

YORK to Inverness

SHEFFIELD to Newton Abbot,

BIRMINGHAM (Sutton Coldfield) to Inverness, Newton Abbot, St. Austell, Stirling

READING to Fishguard, St. Austell

LONDON to Aberdeen, Carmarthen, Carlisle, Edinburgh, Exeter, Fishguard, Newcastle, Newton Abbot, Penzance, Perth, Plymouth, St. Austell, Stirling, Swansea, Totnes

DOVER to Stirling

BRISTOL to Newcastle, Stirling

EXETER to London

CARLISLE to London

NEWTON-LE-WILLOWS to Inverness, Perth, Newton Abbot, St. Austell

CREWE to Inverness

WORCESTER to Totnes, St. Austell

CARMARTHEN to London

FISHGUARD to London, Reading

SWANSEA to London

NEWTON ABBOT to Birmingham, London, Newcastle, Newton-le-Willows, Sheffield, Stirling

ST. AUSTELL to Birmingham, London, Newton-le-Willows, Reading, Worcester

PENZANCE to London, Newcastle

PLYMOUTH to London

TOTNES to London, Worcester

denotes BTH Hotel

Motorail Network, 1972 The map shows all the locations served by Motorail at the height of the service's popularity. There were twenty-six possible destinations in 1972. (Map supplied by Andy Gibbs – zenfolio.com)

Bridge north of Edinburgh in the early morning, we could pull the window down and throw our pennies in the Firth of Forth for good luck. Health and Safety concerns were treated more lightly in those days. Because the Mark 1 sleeping cars were built late in the production run, there were no Mark 2s. The next generation of vehicles were the Mark 3 sleepers built from 1981, so between them the two carriage types will have given sixty years of service when the new stock is introduced in 2018.

Because of the introduction of diesel locomotives, replacing steam power, journey times improved, and by 1962 the night car sleeper left Holloway at the later time of 9.20 p.m. When the West Coast Main Line was electrified as far as Crewe in 1966, the overnight service was given its own station and dedicated loading facility at Kensington Olympia, which was rebuilt with three wide platforms under a new train shed with a reception building, including a waiting room and refreshment facilities. The service was now branded as Motorail, becoming one of British Railways' big success stories, and was well patronised throughout the 1970s. During the 1960s the heavy covered wagons were replaced by the Carflat Wagon, converted from the underframe of former passenger coaches and carrying on average four cars each. There was a brief period of experimentation with double-decker units, when Cartic-4 sets were developed as an efficient way of transporting more cars per wagon. Each set was made up of four wagons, which could hold up to thirty cars. The prototype was built in 1964, and further sets followed in 1966/7. The mix of cars and ground clearance problems meant that they were eventually taken off Motorail duties by 1978, and the service returned to using Carflats.

However, one problem of open trucks was that the diesel engine pulling the train had a tendency to spew diesel oil over the cars during the journey, as John Dawson discovered on a trip from Crewe to Sterling. On arrival he was confronted with cars covered in a thick layer of oil, and was given a small roll of paper towel with which to clean the windscreen. No compensation was offered.

The oldest established Motorail journey is that from York to Inverness, and in its heyday the service ran to and from Harwich, Sutton Coldfield, Newton-le-Willows, Sheffield, St Austell, Newhaven, Dover and Holyhead. Latterly Crewe replaced Newton-le-Willows because of its better passenger amenities. In the mid-1970s it was possible to take your car from Inverness through Crewe to St Austell in Cornwall on a through service – the longest at the time on the network. You could also travel, once a week, between Edinburgh and Bristol, and between Glasgow and Eastbourne, leaving a short drive to the cross-Channel ferries at Newhaven. The Irish seaports were served by Motorail from 1969, connecting Kensington Olympia with the Fishguard–Rosslare sailings, until the Irish Troubles caused a slump in demand. Sometimes

Motorail: You're chauffeur driven all the way
A poster of 1982, encouraging the motorist to 'sleep away the miles', instead of slogging along rain-sodden and congested roads. (Science and Society Picture Library)

the trains were diverted because of weekend engineering works, as Michael Catton remember when he and his wife Roz went off to Scotland on their honeymoon. Normally the train ran up the East Coast Main Line, but on this occasion it went to Edinburgh via Cambridge, which suited them well as they lived in Norfolk and so avoided a long drive to London.

During the era of steam trains, Motorail formations ran at an average speed of 60 mph with a maximum restriction of 75 mph. However, by the 1980s, with Inter-City 125s and 100 mph electric timings, they were struggling to fit in. Motorail trains frequently had to wait on loop lines for the Inter-City 125s to overtake them, and Motorail was beginning to feel like the poor relation. Motorail was also highly labour-intensive, and the densities were low on the sleeper services, so operating costs were high. Shunting engines had to be provided at key stations double-heading was often required and each terminal needed its complement of checking and loading staff. There was also an elaborate reservation system and all this for a limited period during the peak holiday season between Easter and October. As the twentieth century progressed the public were lured away from these islands by package holidays abroad, and with the increase of domestic air travel those on business could travel to and from Scotland more quickly by air Motorail has never been a cheap form of travel and the journey time is no shorter than travelling by car on modern roads.

It was not surprising, therefore, that from a peak of nearly 100,000 cars annually during the 1970s, loadings had fallen to 57,000 in 1981 and parts of the network became unviable. Even so trains still ran from King's Cross to Edinburgh and Aberdeen on the East Coast route, and from Euston to Stirling and Inverness on the West Coast route. A separate service ran from Crewe to Inverness. The Motorail service departed Euston at 10.15 p.m., arriving in Inverness at 9.22 a.m., while the southbound train left Inverness at 7.30 p.m., arriving at Euston at 7.16 a.m. The accompanying publicity brochure encouraged drivers to take out vehicle insurance in case of damage to the car when loading, unloading or in transit.

Soon Kensington Olympia closed for Motorail traffic and standard Inter-City 125 schedule were used to transport passengers while the cars were carried separately on Carflat trains. In 1989 the London–Stirling service was discontinued, and when British Rail was privatised in 1997 the Motorail service ceased completely.

The benefits of Motorail had never really been economic, but were more intangible. An early publicity slogan proclaimed: 'While you sleep, so does your car,' adding, 'no traffic nightmares no pricey petrol.' A later brochure enthused, 'Forget the tension and fatigue of long motorway miles. Just book Motorail and take it easy. With Motorail you're chauffeur-driven all the way.' It was certainly true that you saved on the wear and tear of your car, and on the petrol, over a long road journey, as well as the stresses and hazards of long-distance driving. You arrived at your destination refreshed and relaxed after 'letting the train take the strain'. You also added to the effective length of your holiday by travelling overnight. Sadly the accountants didn't see things that way, and a service that would surely enjoy renewed popularity in the twenty-first century was killed off by railway privatisation.

4

'The Journey of a Night-Time': Travelling the Sleeper Routes

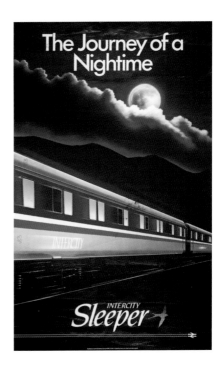

The Journey of a Nightime: Inter-City Sleeper brochure from the 1980s. (Science and Society Picture Library)

To Fort William

The longest through sleeper journey in the British Isles is that between London and Fort William. Dr John McGregor remembers that in the 1950s in the Western Highlands:

> The WH 'Sleeper' with its Kings Cross–Fort William roof boards evoked the awe of any young boy whose idea of a large town was Inverness. That London had not one big station but several could be hard to grasp. On the other hand in faraway London,

a sense of home was to be found, albeit briefly, each evening at King's Cross with the Aberdonian ready to depart – the litany as I recall ran thus: '... the vehicles at the rear are for Fort Willian, calling at Helensburgh Upper, Garelockhead, Arrochar & Tarbet ...'

That this was the WH 'London portion' and not a distinct train made for confusion among less confident travellers. Shunted at Waverley; added to the following Colchester–Glasgow; remarshalling and reversal at Queen Street so as to head the early Glasgow–Mallaig (for easy detachment at Fort William) ... that was the winter timetable norm. Moreover, sitting passengers in the brake-composite now leading, including those who joined in the small hours at Edinburgh, were cut off from breakfast for at least an hour out of Glasgow – until the sleeping car gangway doors were unlocked and access to the buffet-restaurant became possible. But although the sleeping cars and their accompanying brake-composite were officially just an appendage, the combined train was always the 'Sleeper' in popular parlance, a measure of its status in the West Highlands.

The North British Railway 1920
A pictorial poster with Ben Nevis in the centre, showing the 'matchless scenery' of the Western Highlands. (Science and Society Picture Library)

The service had a significance beyond the mere convenience of sleeping one's way from England into the Highlands or vice versa. The 'Sleeper' carried mails for Fort William's second postal delivery, as then was. Besides the 'English post' it brought 'English papers' (and, as I remember, up-market 'English comics' like *The Eagle*). Its timings north and south permitted city exiles in Edinburgh and Glasgow to attend Lochaber funerals on a day-return basis, and such sombre passengers were regularly to be seen. Fort William weddings, first church and then hotel, were set with the southbound 'Sleeper' in mind.

In the 1960s the Aberdonian departed from Platform 1 at London King's Cross at 7.30 p.m. It was headed in those days by a 3,300 hp Deltic diesel-electric locomotive built by the English Electric company. There were often fourteen coaches in the peak holiday and shooting seasons, which would include sleepers for Aberdeen, Dundee and Fort William, and two restaurant cars. King's Cross station, the cavernous terminus of the Great Northern Railway, is a copy of the Czar's Imperial Riding Stables in Moscow, and was a suitably impressive departure point for this stylish named train.

THE NIGHT MAIL

LMS

THE ENGINEMEN

BY SIR WILLIAM ORPEN. R.A.

The Night Mail
An LMS poster of 1924 by Sir William Orpen showing the locomotive crew working hard as the train carries the mails through the night. (Science and Society Picture Library)

Spean Bridge Station
A North British Railway passenger train waits at Spean Bridge station, pulled by Highland Railway No. 93, in around 1900. (Author's Collection)

Fifty years later the Fort William sleeper train starts its journey from another London terminus, Euston, and travels by a different route: the West Coast route. You start at the later time of 9.15 p.m. and follow the London & Birmingham and Grand Junction Railway route, which was first opened by Robert Stephenson in 1838. Unless you are travelling in high summer all will be in darkness by the time you reach Watford Junction, through the deep cutting at Tring, past the old railway workshops at Wolverton and into Kilsby Tunnel, one mile and 666 yards long. The train, powered by a Class 92 electric locomotive built at Crewe, races through Rugby station, on to Crewe itself, home of the railway works and train-spotters' paradise, and then on further north to Preston and Carlisle. The romance of this journey by night was beautifully captured by the famous 1936 film *Night Mail* with poetic words by W. H. Auden, and music by Benjamin Britten.

The poem describes the work of the mail trains to Scotland – post offices on wheels – but it also conjures up the feeling of travelling through the night on a purposeful working train 'pulling up Beattock, shovelling white steam over her shoulder', with people going about their business during the hours of darkness – just the feeling you get on an overnight sleeper. In fact the Highland Sleeper often served as a mail train, as Andrew Haynes recalls only too well from a journey in the 1970s. The Royal Mail compartment wasn't far from his berth, but as the train travelled north he managed to nod off, only to be woken at Peterborough by postal workers yelling at one another and throwing mail bags around. He dozed off again, until they reached Doncaster where he was awakened by more shouts and thuds. So the night progressed with further disruptions at York, Darlington, Durham and Newcastle.

Spean Bridge Station
A passenger train waits at Spean Bridge on the West Highland Line on a sunny day in around 1900. Note the Swiss chalet style station buildings. (Author's Collection)

The West Highland Sleeper waiting to depart from Fort William on Thursday 3 August 2017, headed by a Class 73 locomotive in the new CS livery. (Stuart Vallis)

Whether travelling with the mails or not, once the sleeping passengers reach Edinburgh they may experience a jolt as the electric locomotive is taken off and a Class 67 or 73 diesel is attached to the front of the train during a stationary spell on a remote platform. The air conditioning cuts out and then in again, and all is ready for the onward journey.

The line to Fort William, the West Highland Railway, was first conceived in a mail coach bumping along a rough road from Fort William to Kingussie in the mid-1880s. At that time Kingussie was the nearest railhead, over six hours' drive away. In spite of opposition from the Highland Railway and the Caledonian Railway, the legislation was passed and the first sod was cut on 23 October 1889. The line between Glasgow and Fort William was built in several sections, with about 5,000 navvies being employed at the height of progress. The most challenging section to build was the part of the line that crosses Rannoch Moor, which is wild and remote, and at the summit 1,347 ft above sea level. The moor consisted of spongy peat, moss and heather – a very challenging terrain over which to build a railway line. The contractor John Aird solved the problem by floating the line over layers of turf and brushwood, consolidated by tons of spoil brought from all parts of the system. There were originally fifteen stations, with buildings that looked like miniature Swiss chalets and were painted green.

The gradient is steep as the line leaves Glasgow and heads west alongside the River Clyde. Geoffrey Holliman has lived at Helensburgh for many years, just yards away from the West Highland Line:

The West Highland Sleeper near Loch Treig, on the long climb from Tulloch, at sunset on 21 May 2009. (Norman McNab)

Coming South, 1895, by George Earl
This is the companion painting to *Going North*, and depicts the same group of people on their return journey to London standing on Perth station with their fish, grouse and antlers – trophies of the season. At the time this journey would have taken about twelve hours, and they would almost certainly have been travelling on the overnight sleeper. (Science and Society Picture Library)

Every evening (except Saturday) at 23.18 we hear the sleeper train from Fort William trundling past our house en route to Euston and every morning at approximately 06.45 we hear the north bound service making the return journey. As the train heading for Fort William in the early morning approaches Helensburgh Upper Station via a long uphill gradient, the diesel locomotive always seemed to be straining under the load and the noise and vibration was often my 'wake-up call'. And on some occasions, particularly in wet or snowy weather, the train appeared to have difficulty getting up the hill and would stop, reverse and try again.

As the train pulls up the steep track to Glen Douglas and Garelochhead, passengers are woken with an early call and a pot of tea. The lounge car is serving porridge and bacon rolls, and the view is spectacular. You pass through remote little stations – Crianlarich, Tyndrum and Gorton, which used to be a school station for railway workers' children, and on to Bridge of Orchy. These are wild and desolate regions, full of deer staring incuriously at the train as it trundles past.

Once over the summit of the line at the remote station of Corrour, 1,350 ft above sea level, the train comes into view of Ben Nevis, Britain's highest mountain, and circles the base of the mountain, through Spean Bridge and down the foaming Monessie Gorge, running along the shore of Loch Linnie to Fort William at sea level, where it arrives at 8.20 a.m. When you make the return journey, boarding the small train with its sleeping cars for the trip back down south, the lounge car attendant will happily offer you hotpot or haggis, neeps and tatties, washed down with a splendid assortment of malt whiskies as you watch the sun setting over Rannoch Moor. All is remote, peaceful and feels like another world. Tomorrow morning you will wake to the concrete and bustle of London and the bedlam of the Euston Road.

From Perth to Inverness

The northbound sleeper from Euston crosses the border into Scotland in the early hours of the morning and by the time dawn is breaking during the summer months it is approaching Perth station through the Moncrieffe Tunnel. It is scheduled to arrive at 5.39 a.m., coming to a halt under the much-truncated station roof. The station was designed by Sir William Tite, who also designed Carlisle and Lancaster stations, and was opened in 1847. Its style is best described as mock-Tudor, and its faded glory can be seen to better advantage in George Earl's splendid painting of 1895, *Coming South*, which hangs in the National Railway Museum in York. In the years before the Second World War portions of the rival LMS and LNER sleepers would be remarshalled at Perth to form trains for Aberdeen and Inverness, and at the height of the grouse-shooting season the Inverness train would be run in two or more portions, such was the demand.

There are even stretches of track where you can still hear the trickety-trock sound of unwelded rails.

Beyond Perth the railway follows the River Tay and the A9, following the route of the former Caledonian Railway as far as Stanley Junction, where the line becomes single track. We then travel on the Highland Railway proper, past the old county asylum at Murthly, skirting the edge of Birnam Wood with its Shakespearean associations, and entering the cathedral town of Dunkeld. Beatrix Potter, the writer of the Peter Rabbit books for children, came on holiday in 1892 to Birnam, where their holiday accommodation overlooked the station, and she reported in her journal that, 'The trains prove to be a source of constant amusement. Papa is constantly running out, and looks out of the bedroom window at night.'

A fine viaduct designed by Joseph Mitchell carries the railway over the Tay, at Dalguise, and we are soon approaching Ballinluig where we join the River Tummel, which leads us along

Inverness Station
HR No. 145 waits to depart from Inverness station in around 1900, while carriages occupy the other platforms. The cupola of the Station Hotel is visible above the platform canopy. (Author's Collection)

The Sleeper stands at the platform at Inverness just before departure south to London on 2 August 2017. Note the new CS livery on the seating coach. (Stuart Vallis)

A poster of 1920 showing the extent of the Highland Railway lines and advertising the quickest route to the Highlands via Perth and Dunkeld. (Science and Society Picture Library)

the valley, climbing steadily to Pitlochry (arrival time 6.16 a.m.) with its handsome station in the Scots Tudor Style. We continue climbing towards Killiecrankie, a famous beauty spot on the River Garry, crossing the ten-arch viaduct before entering a short tunnel. After Blair Atholl the train faces a long climb towards Druimuachdar Summit (1,484 ft above sea level), bidding farewell to the Vale of Atholl and entering the rugged terrain of the Grampian Mountains. In the days of steam traction this stretch would need a pair of Black Fives or a banking engine pushing from the rear of the train. We pass the remains of Dalnaspidal station, once the highest station on the British main lines but which closed in 1965.

Having crossed the watershed we pick up and follow the River Truim, passing Dalwhinnie, reputedly Scotland's highest village, with its whisky distillery which opened in 1898. The line now drops down into Glen Truim, where the river becomes the Spey, and we pass through Newtonmore, then Kingussie and Kincraig, passing the monument to the

---

72

INVERNESS.

The Highland Railway Company's
STATION HOTEL.

Patronised by their Royal Highnesses the Prince and Princess of Wales,
the Duke of Cambridge Prince and Princess Christian,
and other Members of the Royal Family, and by most of the Nobility of Europe.

This Large and Handsome Hotel, adjoining the Station, with all the modern Improvements, and elegantly Furnished, is acknowledged to be one of the best appointed in the Kingdom. Has recently undergone extensive Additions and Alterations, and contains numerous Suites of comfortable and lofty Apartments. A new elegant Coffee-room, Drawing-room Smoking and Billiard-rooms, Lavatories, and Bath rooms.

Pianos are at the free disposal of the occupants in every Private Sitting-room.

Parties leaving in the morning can go over the grand Scenery along the Skye Railway, or visit either Loch-Maree, Gairloch, Dunrobin, or Golspie, and return the same day to the Hotel.

Table d'Hôte at 6.30 and 7.30; on Sundays at 5 p.m. only.

AN OMNIBUS ATTENDS THE STEAMERS.
Hotel Porters Attend at the Station.
POSTING

TARIFF:

Sitting-rooms—Ground Floor, per Day 5s	Luncheons and Suppers—Cold Meat 1s 6d	
Do. —1st Floor . 7s 6d to 10s	Soup . . . . . 1s and 1s 6d	
Bedrooms—1st „ . . 3s 6d	Dinners—From the Joints . 2s 6d	
Do. —2nd „ . . 3s 0d	Soups, Fish, Entrées, &c., &c., as per daily bill	
Do. —3rd „ . . 2s 6d	of fare, at proportionally moderate charges.	
If two Persons occupy one Bed, 1s extra.	Table d'Hôte 4s 6d	
Board—Plain Breakfasts & Teas. 1s 6d	Special Dinners in Private Sitting-	
Do., with Cold Meat or Broiled	Rooms from 5s	
Ham 2s	A large assortment of choice Wines as per	
Do., with Chops or White Fish, 2s 6d	List.	
Do., with Salmon, Steak, or		
Ham and Eggs, or Chicken	Fires—Sitting-room, 1s 6d ; Bedroom, 1s.	
with Ham and Tongue 3s	Baths—Hot, 1s 6d ; Cold, 1s ; Hip or	
Table d'Hôte Breakfast . . 3s	Sponge, 6d.	
Service—A charge of 1s 6d per day will be made to Visitors occupying Rooms. In other cases, 3d per Meal.		

A Large Comfortable Room is provided for Commercial Gentlemen.

EDWARD CESARI, Manager.

Station Hotel, Inverness Build in the Italianate style in the 1850s, the Station Hotel, now renamed the Royal Highland Hotel, has welcomed weary travellers for over 150 years.

It originally had a private entrance from the railway station, and in the 1880s the manager, Edward Cesari, could boast that it was patronised by royalty. Over the years it became something of a Highland institution. (Science and Society Picture Library)

Right: The Royal Highland Hotel today, formerly the Station Hotel, and still an important destination for travellers to the north of Scotland. (Stuart Vallis)

Below: David, one of the sleeping car attendants, on the platform at Inverness, on 25 May 2017, wearing the new CS uniform. (Author's Collection)

The Sleeper waiting to depart Inverness on 26 May 2017. (Author's Collection)

LMS   **INVERNESS**   **LNER**

by NORMAN WILKINSON RI

A panoramic view of Inverness and the Ness River by Norman Wilkinson on a 1930s poster for the LMS and LNER. (Science and Society Picture Library)

Duke of Gordon, and one to the Gordon Highlanders who fell at the Battle of Waterloo. Soon we pull into the beautifully restored station at Aviemore, designed by Murdoch Patterson and opened in 1898. At 7.43 a.m. (arrival time) we are probably drinking a cup of tea or tucking into an early breakfast in the lounge car. In any case, there is plenty to look at from the train, especially the sight of the Strathspey Railway, which runs trains between Aviemore and Broomhill via Boat of Garten.

Leaving the Spey Valley behind, the train climbs through woodland with distant views of Cairn Gorm towards its second major summit at Slochd, 1,315 ft above sea level. The line then drops down towards the village of Tomatin, with its whisky distillery, and traverses the valley on the graceful Findhorn Viaduct, a steel girder structure supported on tapering masonry piers. After this the line runs steadily downhill towards Inverness. At Daviot station, closed in 1965, we join the River Nairn, and the railway track doubles again. There are distant views westwards of the Moray and Beauly firths and the mountains beyond. We cross the massive twenty-nine-arch sandstone viaduct, 600 yards long, at Culloden, over the River Nairn, and pass the sight of the famous battle in 1746 when the Jacobite forces under Charles Stuart (Bonnie Prince Charlie) were defeated by the Duke of Cumberland. It was

Tay Bridge
British Railways poster of 1957 by Terence Cuneo. (Science and Society Picture Library)

the last significant military battle fought on British soil. Soon we are entering the suburbs of Inverness as the line goes over the line to Aberdeen at Milburn Junction, where there are sidings, railway maintenance facilities and an array of diesel engines and snowploughs. Here too is the old Highland Railway's Lochgorm Works, now the maintenance depot for the Caledonian Sleeper fleet. Inverness station dates from 1855, and is Y-shaped, with the lines from Perth coming in from the east, while the Far North Line to Thurso and Wick comes in from the north-west. In years gone by the sleeper would travel round the connecting Rose Street curve of the triangular layout and reverse into the station so that passengers could walk across the platform to the trains for Thurso, Wick and Kyle of Lochalsh. Today the engine pulls us slowly into the platform at 8.38 a.m., and our journey to Inverness is over. Just beyond the station concourse is the former Station Hotel, now the Royal Highland Hotel, built in the 1850s in an Italianate style and forming one side of Station Square in the heart of the city, and no doubt a welcome sight to weary travellers on their journeys north and south.

From Edinburgh to Aberdeen

Aberdeen is the largest town on the east coast of Scotland between Dundee and Inverness, and has long been a centre of commerce for the area. In the mid-nineteenth century railway promoters cast greedy eyes northwards to push lines from Perth to Aberdeen, while others favoured the coastal route via Dundee. The railway to Perth, from Edinburgh and Glasgow, was opened on 22 May 1848 and finally reached Aberdeen in April 1850. The route was

A view from the sleeper over the countryside near Aberdeen on 2 August 2017. (Stuart Vallis)

Royal Highlander Approaches Aberdeen
A poster by Norman Wilkinson for the LMS in 1923 shows the maroon-liveried train running along the stretch of line between Stonehaven and Aberdeen. (Science and Society Picture Library)

a combination of several railway companies, but eventually all were amalgamated with the Caledonian Railway. Once the first Tay Bridge had been built in 1877, the second Tay Bridge in 1887, and the Forth Bridge opened in 1890, it became possible to send express and goods trains between Aberdeen and London.

Those who have travelled north from London will be beginning to stir in their berths as the train leaves Waverley station and heads north through Haymarket and Dalmeny. Soon we are rumbling slowly over the iconic Forth Bridge, recently repainted at a cost of £130 million. As the train passes over the bridge between the 12-ft tubes and criss-crossing girders, we can look down to the Firth of Forth some 150 ft below. We pass North Queensferry and at Inverkeithing leave the Perth main line and briefly hug the coast, where we can see Inchcolm Island, home to a twelfth-century abbey. At Burntisland we run past a magnificent stretch of sandy beach, and then on to Kirkcaldy, Cupar, Leuchars Junction and the waters of the Firth of Tay. Unlike the Forth Bridge, the Tay Bridge is only a

No. 73971 waits at Aberdeen having hauled the sleeper from Edinburgh on 2 August 2017. (Stuart Vallis)

moderate height above the sea, but it is two miles long, sweeping in a gentle curve into Tay Bridge station in Dundee, city of marmalade and D. C. Thomson, publisher of *The Beano*.

Beyond Dundee the line follows the coast through Broughty Ferry, Carnoustie, with its golf courses and a distant glimpse of the Inchcape Rock, and on to Arbroath, where smoked haddock is a speciality. There are wonderful panoramic views over Lunan Bay as the train tackles the steep gradient approaching Lunan Bay station. We travel on the viaduct across the harbour at Montrose with a view of the tall spire of the parish church, and then leave the coast and climb to Kinaber Junction, the famous winning post of the Race to the North in 1895. Then comes the final run downhill over seven miles into Aberdeen, and at Ferryhill Junction we slow down for the last half mile into Aberdeen station. The station was built between 1913 and 1916, replacing a structure of 1867, and enables passengers to connect directly with the lines to the north. The buildings were incorporated in the Union Square development in the early twenty-first century and the sandstone building became the centrepiece of a covered plaza with shops and station offices. We have arrived at what was once the final destination of the Flying Scotsman, a journey which in the 1920s took over twelve hours from King's Cross, arriving at about 10 p.m. This time, however, we can leave the comfort of our sleeping berth, refreshed with a light breakfast, and walk along the platform into the 'granite city' soon after 7.30 a.m., ready for the day ahead.

'Anything is Possible on a Train': Stories from the Sleepers

The author and broadcaster Ludovic Kennedy summed up the romance of the Anglo-Scottish sleepers very well in his introduction to *A Book of Railway Journeys (Collins 1980)*:

> My own affection for them began as a small boy when travelling to the Scottish Highlands for summer holidays before the war. Then, as now, the delight lay in the unaccustomed break with routine – the bustle of the terminus, porters jostling for the bags: stocking up with literature and chocolate at the platform stalls: then, settled in, the long, sweet wait for the whistle and the slow inching forward to the north. Dinner and a fitful sleep, and in the morning a bedside window on another world: deer on the hill-side, wind on the heather, the heart of Scotland at my feet.

Kennedy goes on to say that while in the days when train travel was the norm, we tended to take it for granted, now, after years of flirting with motorway and air travel, we are rediscovering the comparative delights of the train. Kennedy points out that we can move around in a train, look out of the windows, strike up a conversation, have something to eat, and all with our luggage nearby. But almost the greatest pleasure is in the anticipation of the journey and the people we might meet. 'Train travel, being contracted both in time and space, magnifies character, intensifies relationships, unites the disparate.' People become more confiding, secure in the knowledge that they probably won't meet again. In that spirit here are some stories from some of the many thousands who have used the Anglo-Scottish sleepers over the years, and whose experiences make the sleeper such a richly satisfying mode of travel.

Some Enchanted Evening

Sheena Crane recalls two encounters when, in her early twenties, she travelled north to her home in Argyll on the Euston–Glasgow sleeper in the 1970s. When the steward brought

Southbound Fort William–London Euston Sleeper passing the head of Loch Treig, between Tulloch and Corrour, on the evening of 21 May 2009. (Norman McNab)

The Northbound London–Fort William Sleeper has just crossed the Rannoch viaduct north of Rannoch station on the morning of 7 January 2010. Note: it was running over one hour late due to iced points. The air temperature at the time was -12 C. (Norman McNab)

her a cup of tea she got into a conversation, and he mentioned that he had been a prisoner of war in Japan during the Second World War. He returned later, sat down, and began to share his POW experiences. Sheena was young and sympathetic, which encouraged him to tell her about the terrible things he and his fellow prisoners suffered, and how he would always remember the bravery of his colleagues who didn't return.

On another occasion, travelling south to London, Sheena got into conversation in the lounge car with a soldier from a Scottish regiment:

> We chatted with others until late, when, just as I was saying good-night, he took me aside and asked me if I would be able to accompany him to Buckingham Palace the next day – where he was being presented to HM The Queen and given an award.
>
> Although surprised, I was very touched and explained that I had just met the man I wanted to marry and I wasn't sure he would be very happy if I accepted his very kind offer. Especially as he was meeting me at Euston in the morning.
>
> Looking back, of course I wish I had – and my husband-to-be would have been perfectly happy.
>
> Even worse, I can't remember what he said his award was for – but I vaguely remember I was very impressed.
>
> In the morning, when I left the train, I saw him disembark in his full-dress uniform – and I knew immediately I should have said yes, and accompanied him to the Palace.
>
> I've always regretted my decision and hoped that the wonderful occasion and the recognition for his service was compensation for having nobody to accompany him...

Elspeth and Jim Edwards fondly recall their journeys on the sleeper to Fort William for walking holidays, always in February, when there were no tourists around. Over the years they have gathered a group of like-minded friends and 2017 marked their twenty-first trip north with eight others. They have got the embarkation down to a fine art: always first in the queue to check in with the sleeping car attendant, followed by a quick dash down the platform to bag seats in the lounge car. After the 'Edinburgh Shunt' it was always gratifying to be hauled by a diesel locomotive on the final leg – Class 37 'Growlers' until their replacement by the Class 67 'Cyclops'. They never forget a cheery wave to the widow of a railwayman who lives in a bungalow beside the line at Roy Bridge Station, and who invariably waves back.

Romance has never been far away on the sleeper either. In August 1925, at the start of the grouse season, Marmaduke Furness, the 1st Viscount Furness, a Yorkshire shipbuilder, colliery owner and iron and steel proprietor, invited Thelma Converse, daughter of an American diplomat, to join the party at his shooting lodge near Inverness. They travelled up by the night sleeper, together with his staff, a valet, three footmen and two housemaids. Thelma had barely settled into her compartment before the valet knocked and informed her that dinner was ready. She found her host waiting in a sleeping compartment, which his staff had converted into a temporary private dining room, with white tablecloth, champagne in an ice bucket and a picnic hamper packed with all kinds of delicacies. '"What, no plovers' eggs?" she asked, at which he took her in his arms and told her he loved her – a carefully planned stratagem, with a predictable outcome.' (*The Long Weekend*:

The West Highland Sleeper crossing Rannoch Moor as the sun sets on 3 August 2017. (Stuart Vallis)

Adrian Tinniswood: Jonathan Cape: p. 275.) They married the next year, but that marriage came to an end when she began an affair with Edward, Prince of Wales (later Edward VIII) in 1933.

That story shows that the overnight sleeper has always been a romantic rendezvous and a place for fleeting liaisons full of excitement, promise and sometimes illicit attraction. Occasionally, though, things can go embarrassingly wrong. On one journey north there was a lively crowd of people in the lounge car, enjoying sampling the range of whiskies long into the evening. One female passenger took a fancy to a man she had been talking to over a dram or two and, after he had retired to his cabin, she soon followed and knocked on his door. They settled down together and she stayed on in his compartment. Unfortunately, when she woke the next morning she discovered that she was in the wrong portion of the train. The Highland sleeper had divided overnight, and she found herself in Aberdeen, while her puzzled husband was waiting on the platform at Fort William, somewhat irate that his wife had not arrived, while her luggage had. History does not record how she got out of that awkward situation, but 'stick to your own cabin' seems to be the moral of the story!

However, the sleeper has also been the scene of more lasting romances, and the start of more than one honeymoon. Sally-Jane Coode met her husband-to-be on a sleeper, and they celebrated their fiftieth wedding anniversary by travelling on the Paddington–Penzance sleeper train. Clifford Bevan, at the time a member of the band The Temperance Seven, spent his honeymoon in Scotland and travelled back to London on the Night Scotsman.

And the sleeper has nearly witnessed the birth of a baby, but thankfully help arrived just in time. Pippa Fell takes up the story:

We were returning on the Sleeper to London from our cottage near Fort William in November 2015 when my waters broke some five weeks prematurely just south of Glasgow. Calling my midwife in London I was told I needed to get to hospital quick smart so my husband Simon, looking rather pale, hot-footed it to find the guard and ask if we could stop the train...

The next available (non-scheduled stop) was Lockerbie and the driver was given permission to get us there at breakneck speed. In the meantime the train manager on duty, a lovely lady named Shona, appeared to ask how I was faring, revealing by the happiest of happenstances that she was a retired district nurse!

She and the team arranged for an ambulance to meet the train, brought water, supplies and reassurance and tracked our progress on Google Maps until we got there. Lockerbie station was dwarfed by the Sleeper as it rattled to a halt and the ambulance men were waiting right by our door as we arrived. We and our bags were helped off by the Sleeper team and our daughter was born safely later that day.

Return from Honeymoon
Clifford Bevan's wife, standing beside the Night Scotsman on the last night of their honeymoon on 2 September 1961. Notice the phantom Scotsman standing in the corridor. (Clifford Bevan)

As regular travellers we still see the team who helped us that night, and we tell our daughter how special they are!

Too Close for Comfort

Over the years many strangers must have slept in close proximity to each other, as they shared the Second Class sleeping cabins, one above the other. Never very popular, this could sometimes give rise to amusing or uncomfortable encounters. Michael Griffey remembers sharing a Glasgow–Euston sleeper with a Scotsman whose only piece of luggage was a small cardboard suitcase. As the train left he opened it to reveal a bottle of whisky and several cans of beer. After a convivial evening, they turned in and Michael slept soundly, to be awakened with 'breakfast' consisting of the remains of his companion's suitcase.

John Allen recalls another Glasgow–London journey when he ended up on the bottom bunk. His fellow traveller was already tucked up above with his shoes nicely laid out underneath John's bunk...

> Lights out came fairly soon, and in reply to my 'Goodnight' he gave me a short summary of his Friday night out which involved a few pints and a curry, which he said would enable him to sleep well. I, as usual, had a pretty rough sleep and awoke at Crewe, at which time my fellow traveller's digestive system kicked in! A horrendous smell filled the tight space, though I did find some respite by wedging one of his shoes in the door to give me some fresh air. Such are the dubious joys of night-time travel, though I am always pulled back to the Sleeper.

Women in particular can feel anxious if they have chosen to share a cabin, and always secretly hope that the second berth will remain unoccupied. Anne Harper remembers the frightened face that greeted her as she entered her cabin: 'Oh, thank goodness you're a woman! By the way, I had my bath before I came.' Ian Tegner was told a story by a family friend, Barbara, who was travelling to Oban to meet her husband during the Second World War, when there was no segregation of the sexes in the four-berth compartments. Finding that the other three berths were booked by men, Barbara quickly established herself on the top bunk, and when the three men entered the cabin she pretended to be fast asleep. After a short while there was a tap on her shoulder and one of the men said: 'My dear, if you don't look now you will never again see three bishops without their gaiters.'

Even when two women are sharing a cabin there can be unforeseen hazards. Trish Reeves recounts the following experience:

> I was travelling up to Scotland to take part in a sailing course. Travelling Second Class on the sleeper I had to share with another lady, but having arrived early I had established myself in the bottom bunk. In the morning I opened my eyes to find her false teeth grinning at me on my pillow. I wasn't sure what the etiquette was for such a situation so I didn't say anything, got up quietly, and left them lying where I found them. When the lady above me discovered what had happened she was most

embarrassed and apologetic, but being British I pretended this was a perfectly normal occurrence and we parted on good terms.

Audrey Rivet recalls catching the Inverness sleeper at Crewe, aged nineteen, in 1944. She and her father hadn't booked, but the guard found them each a berth. She was pushed into a four-berth cabin containing three RAF officers in various states of undress, one dangling his legs over the edge of the top bunk wearing blue and white striped underpants, and looking very embarrassed, as was she. Just then the door slid open and the guard pulled her out. In the meantime he had pushed her father into a cabin with three WRAF officers! All was sorted out, and as Audrey peered out of the window she could see a WRAF officer marching down the dimly lit platform, complaining that the bunk she was expecting was not available. She describes waking at dawn and seeing the wild scenery of the Highlands, a truly wonderful experience for a girl who had never been north of Birmingham.

One of the problems with ticketing systems is that they occasionally cause confusion about gender. In an interview in *The Gramophone* the English bass-baritone John Shirley-Quirk reported his experience on a London–Edinburgh sleeper in the 1970s. On entering his Second Class cabin he found an attractive young lady on one of the bunks, because he had been listed as 'Miss Shirley Quirk'. Sadly, he recalled that he was swiftly relocated. In January 2000 the Revd Canon Gwyneth Evans decided to treat herself to a holiday in Scotland, starting with the Caledonian Sleeper. Presenting herself to the female attendant at Euston, she was informed that she would be sharing her cabin, so she asked for an upgrade. The attendant consulted her list and asked 'Are you the Revd Evans?' to which she replied that she was. 'Oh,' came the response, 'I assumed you were a man, so I have put you in with a man.' Gwyneth brightly replied, 'Maybe my luck's changed!' At this the attendant drew herself up to her full height and exclaimed, 'Madam, it's too late for that!' Gwyneth did so hope it was the lateness of the hour to which she referred...

When Things Go Wrong...

Happily, most sleeper journeys are uneventful and we reach our destination more or less on time, as planned. The memorable occasions are often those when something goes wrong. Captain Nick Kettlewell RN remembers a journey to Glasgow nearly fifty years ago:

When I was the Senior Naval Officer at the old Fairfield shipyard in Govan waiting for a destroyer to be built I regularly travelled back to Glasgow on a Sunday night in the sleeper train that also included the Pullman Night Bar. In February 1970 it was so cold that buses were stopped in the street as their diesel was frozen. At 4 a.m. one Monday morning the train stopped unexpectedly at Beattock station and I observed railwaymen on the platform. I put on my overcoat and alighted to ask what the problem was. The train ahead of us had broken down about a mile up the track. I asked what was to be done? It was clear that this was their problem. Our engine driver and guard were there and so I suggested that we took our train up and hauled the casualty back to Beattock. Its passengers could then be disembarked and we would push their train into a siding (which fortunately still existed). We would then draw back into the platform, embark the passengers and head to Glasgow.

They had no idea who I was but liked my plan so I suggested they telephone the signalman and put it into effect. Thus we all got to Glasgow without freezing to death at Beattock!

The authoritative presence of a naval officer clearly saved the day on that occasion, but others could be resourceful too. Pippa Brown was travelling south from Fort William, but on approaching Rannoch Moor at about 10 p.m. the train became slower and slower and finally ground to a halt at Tulloch.

The driver announced that they were going no further as it would take five hours to rescue us with another engine, and he had no intention of getting us marooned for the night on Rannoch Moor! But the lovely lady in charge of the lounge car filled us up with sandwiches and drams as we had no idea how long we would be stationary. However, a good-tempered coach driver was summoned from his supper and we caught up with the sleeper from Inverness which was held for us at Dalwhinnie. It was just like John Buchan with the train puffing gently to itself, and, as it was midnight, everyone else asleep. Bunks were found for us, and we left Dalwhinnie in a very cheerful mood! What is more we arrived back at Euston on time the next day.

Sometimes the sleepers do get delayed and fall well behind schedule. Sandy Sullivan was returning to London from Edinburgh, and agreed that his travelling companion should get up first in the morning because of his tighter schedule. Sometime about 6.00 a.m. they both awoke to the familiar sounds of a busy railway station, and his companion rose, shaved, dressed and said farewell. He returned a few minutes later to report that the train had been delayed in the night, and that they were only at Newcastle.

Even worse, Colin Brown remembers a journey to Glasgow in December 1956:

When I arrived at Euston Station there was an announcement that trains were delayed by fog. I thought this odd since it was a clear evening and I had no problem with the journey from Chelmsford to Liverpool Street. The train came into the platform about half an hour after its scheduled departure time, but after settling into my four-berth shared cabin, the train seemed to move off fairly sharply. I remember thinking – well this isn't going to be too bad – and I fell asleep.

Around eight o'clock in the morning I woke up and realised that the train had stopped and I looked out into the murky light to see that we were adjacent to a large marshalling yard. I could see it wasn't Glasgow, so I rather hoped it might be Carlisle. As the train moved off into the station I was appalled to find that we were only at Crewe!

We were served breakfast – a cup of tea and two tea biscuits! There were no other catering arrangements on the train.

After many hours of tedium and dire hunger we finally arrived at Glasgow Central about 5.30 p.m. A tad late after a twenty-hour journey!

Michael Spencer arrived on the platform at Kirkcaldy station only to be told that the sleeper from Aberdeen was stuck behind an accident involving a large lorry and a railway bridge. A taxi had been laid on to take him and his wife to Edinburgh, where they joined other passengers who had been bussed in from Aberdeen, Dundee and Stonehaven. A replacement sleeper had been laid on, and they were eventually led to it. Unfortunately, his wife, in walking boots and rucksack, got caught up in a rowdy gang of Glaswegians whom the police were shovelling into the last train home. Thinking she was one of the party, they tried to throw her into the Glasgow train too. When she explained she was going for the sleeper, a burly policeman said, 'The sleeper's long gone, cully,' and began rattling his handcuffs. She was eventually delivered to the relief sleeper, even more hot and bothered than before.

Caroline M. tells of an incident when her sister was travelling on the London–Inverness sleeper and was due to get off at Pitlochry where she was joining the family for a holiday. The custom was to leave a car at the station which guests would then use to get to their house, avoiding very early morning drives to collect visitors. On this occasion her sister didn't arrive at the expected time, only turning up a couple of hours later. She explained that she had overslept, because the attendant hadn't brought her an early morning cup of tea and a reminder about her destination. She only realised what was happening when the train was pulling out of Pitlochry station, so she pulled the communication cord. The train ground to a halt about half a mile down the line and she, having hastily dressed, opened a carriage door, jumped down onto the track and walked back to the station. There was, naturally, consternation on the train and she was given a heavy fine, which she refused to pay, on the grounds that the attendant failed to knock on her cabin door. Because the driver had to release the brakes on all the carriages the train was several hours late, and no doubt the other passengers were furious.

The next story in this section on the perils and pitfalls of sleeper travel comes from the management. Gerard Fiennes was a railway manager who rose through the ranks to become Chief Operating Officer of British Rail in 1961–63 and later General Manager of BR's Eastern Region.

He was fired from British Rail in 1967 for publishing the book *I Tried to Run a Railway* which was outspoken about the management of the railways. In a subsequent book, *Fiennes on Rails* (David & Charles, 1986), he recounts an incident when travelling north on the sleeper as General Manager of the Eastern Region. He entitled it 'Lost Property', and in it he describes how he was woken up by the attendant, who had with him a lady wearing a skimpy nightdress who claimed to have lost her husband. It turned out that they were in adjacent First Class sleeping cabins with the inter-connecting door open. When she awoke in the middle of the night she saw that her husband wasn't there. Having searched for him in vain she sought help from the attendant, who roused Gerard Fiennes from sleep. Fiennes realised that this might be a tricky situation, pulled on a macintosh over his pyjamas and went in search of the missing husband. Meanwhile, the wife had tucked herself up in Fiennes' bed. He tracked down Sam, the lounge bar attendant, who told Fiennes exactly which cabin the husband was in, but on arriving back at his own cabin he bumped into said husband, who complained, 'I've lost my wife!' Then he saw her in Fiennes' bed, she jumped up and off they went. Fiennes thought the husband would be none too pleased, but when they met at the ticket barrier in the morning he grasped Fiennes' arm and said, 'Thanks a million, old chap!'

And finally in this section, an experience that happened to me only last year when travelling from Inverness to Euston. The train had just left the station and we were settling down in the lounge car with a drink when our worried-looking attendant came through asking if anyone claimed a piece of unidentified luggage in the next coach. No one spoke, so she hurried through to the sitting coach, only to come back and ask again more urgently. Finally someone realised it might be theirs and was asked to identify it, so all was well. But the attendant told me later that, in the wake of the Manchester bombing and consequent heightened security, if the case had been unclaimed they would have had to stop and evacuate the train.

Early the next morning, after waiting for a long time at Penrith, we were informed that a goods train had brought down the power lines near Preston and we could not proceed any further. Eventually the train backed into Carlisle and we were decanted on to the platform at 6.30 a.m., with no breakfast. A coach was promised to take us to Preston, but some of us took the early train to Newcastle and caught an East Coast train to King's Cross, arriving five and a half hours late. This incident was entirely beyond the control of the Caledonian Sleeper, but shows that when things do go wrong, they can go wrong disastrously and cause great inconvenience.

Animals on Trains

The railways have a set of carefully worked out regulations when it comes to transporting animals in railway carriages, allowing passengers to take dogs, cats and other small animals with them 'so long as they do not endanger or inconvenience passengers or staff'. The Caledonian Sleeper now allows guide dogs on board in single cabins, and other dogs are allowed subject to an extra charge for a heavy duty clean. When dogs travel in the guard's van they must be secured with a collar and be properly muzzled.

However, in years gone by the regulations were much stricter. A notice in *Bradshaw's Timetable for the East Coast Sleepers* in 1961 firmly states: 'Dogs or other livestock are not allowed to be taken into the sleeping cars.'

When Stanley Lowy and his wife took their Welsh Border Collie Lisa on the Car Sleeper to Stirling, the attendant insisted that Lisa should travel in the guard's van. Lisa wasn't very happy, but settled on a familiar rug that they provided. Early next morning there was a knock on the compartment door, which they thought heralded tea and biscuits, but was in fact the guard who requested their urgent presence in the guard's van 'to see to your dog'. Lisa greeted them enthusiastically, and the guard said, 'That dog should have been muzzled!' Apparently at Berwick-upon-Tweed, Lisa, who had taken upon herself the task of guarding a pile of *Times* newspapers, refused to allow the station staff to off-load the papers, no doubt expecting her owners to deal with them. Stanley sends belated apologies to the good burghers of Berwick for the lack of their favourite paper that day.

In the days of the old Third Class four-berth sleepers Anne Pelham Burn remembers her mother exclaiming, 'This isn't fit for a dog!' as she climbed into her scratchy, smelly moquette bunk with its rough blanket on the King's Cross–Aberdeen sleeper. On her return home she commissioned a joiner to make up a Second Class sleeper box for two dogs, both terriers. He made a wooden box, divided in half, one up, one underneath, with a roof on

STUDIO SEVEN

Please remember...

my ticket...

a new scale of charges for
accompanied dogs has been introduced BRITISH RAILWAYS

Please Remember
My Ticket
A BR poster from
the 1950s reminding
passengers about
the new charges for
taking accompanied
dogs on the train.
(Science and Society
Picture Library)

top, each bed provided with a luxurious doggy cushion upon which the terriers reclined in perfect comfort for the rest of their days. It was known as 'The Sleeper'.

Smaller pets were more easily portable, and could travel in the sleeping compartment, but this could cause problems. Sandi Holton remembers a journey from Kirkcaldy to London with a pet hamster:

I was in the top bunk of the sleeper and installed the hamster in his cage at the end of the bunk by my feet when I got into the sleeping compartment in Kirkcaldy. The bottom bunk occupant, a charming lady, got on in Edinburgh, and as she entered the compartment I hastily covered the hamster cage with my coat. We chatted away as the train drew out of the station. But! Being night time the hamster was soon busy scrabbling around his cage and spinning on his wheel. She stopped chatting and asked if I had heard a funny noise? Noise, no I replied longing for the train to gather speed and start rattling over the tracks. And so it began ... my long night of trying to keep a hamster quiet. When the night attendant passed by the Edinburgh lady had him listening too but fortunately to no avail. He winked at me as if to say what is that all about and I colluded with him raising my hands as if questioning the poor woman's sanity! I quietly took the hamster out of his cage from time to time when the noise got too much and tried to hold him, but my next nightmare was him escaping or falling into the bottom bunk, the cord being pulled and the train stopped by my companion! Finally I had to quietly remove the wheel from his cage and that helped. The next morning my companion was in no hurry to leave the train so I was forced to wait while she unhurriedly prepared herself for London, and her last words to the sleeping car attendant were to the effect that there seemed to be a mouse in the walls of the train. I was finally able to go off with my hamster and cage unobserved but it was certainly a memorable journey.

The writer and conservationist Beatrix Potter, best known for her Peter Rabbit children's books, described in her journal a journey by sleeper from King's Cross to Edinburgh and on to Perth in July 1892 when she took her pet rabbit along with her:

Tuesday, July 26th – Left London with East Coast and Forth Bridge, 7.30 pm King's Cross. Stopped only at Grantham, York, Newcastle, Berwick, and a wayside station before reaching Edinburgh at a repulsively chilly, unearthly hour. The light came in this instance near Berwick and was broad daylight, but cold and damp when we stopped through some delay near Dunbar, opposite a sleeping station garden full of rose bushes weighed down with wet.

Benjamin Bunny travelled in a covered basket in the wash-place; took him out of the basket near Dunbar, but proved scared and bit the family. Not such a philosophical traveller as poor Spot [the family dog, who had died earlier that year].

Pets often don't appreciate travelling in cars or trains, as Michael Binyon discovered in 1962. Having lived in Northern Ireland he was moving with his family back to England, and took the ferry crossing from Larne to Stranraer. They then caught the night train from Stranraer, which in those days ran through Dumfries to Carlisle and on to London. They had sent ahead all their furniture and just took hand luggage with them. The only problem was their budgerigar. It couldn't go with the furniture and couldn't be left behind, so they took it in the sleeping compartment with them. Unfortunately the sleeping carriage rocked and rolled throughout the night and the budgerigar was swinging wildly in its cage, back and forth, all night long. By the next morning it was lying on the bottom of the cage, unable to fly and barely able to walk. It recovered... eventually.

The School Run

Many people, especially those who have used the sleepers regularly, retain fond memories of the service. This is particularly true for those whose sleeper experiences began in childhood.

John Savery recalls that getting overexcited very young children to go to sleep on a night train could be quite a challenge.

> One solution was to explain to them that 'this is a sleeper train and it cannot go until all the passengers, particularly children, are asleep'. That story is believable as the train remains in the station well after most children's normal bed time. Clearly the train is waiting for them to go to sleep! If the children are still awake when the train does start moving they think that everyone else must be asleep and they had better keep very quiet in case they are found out and stop the train!

Lyn Austin remembers travelling with her sister (aged ten and eleven), unaccompanied from London to Aberdeen in August 1958.

> We loved our cabin – it was luxurious – with a cupboard in the corner by the window which hid a little sink. It was all very exciting and once the journey started we tried to stay awake as long as we could. We must have got some sleep because the guard woke us around dawn letting us know that the train was approaching the Forth Bridge. On arrival at Aberdeen we were met by our cousins who took us to Auntie Mina's farm near Keith for our holiday.

Mary Baker recalls taking the sleeper from Edinburgh to King's Cross, aged thirteen, in 1950, on her way back to boarding school in England:

> The trouble was I was accompanied by my cello which took up all the room on the top bunk. I was so scared of hurting it I had to sleep on the outer edge of the bunk, only held in by the vertical straps. Being brought tea and biscuits by the guard in the morning was the height of luxury. On arrival I found myself a porter and trekked back to the guard's van, still clutching my cello, to get my school trunk. Then we all walked over to The Station Hotel where cello and I sat in the lounge, having been instructed to order milk and porridge, while I waited to be collected by a lady from Universal Aunts for the onward journey to Paddington.

Margaret Brown remembers frequent trips by First Class sleeper from Arbroath or Perth to King's Cross between 1951 and 1959 to enable her to get to school in Hertfordshire:

> Getting into a nightie, washing my teeth in my own little basin, using the potty underneath, and most important of all, hanging my wristwatch on the hook above a special chamois leather cushion – all became the normal pattern at the beginning and end of term. I was even treated occasionally to dinner by officers from HMS *Condor*, Arbroath, with a full three course meal and silver service. Sometimes I helped the steward take round the morning tea and biscuits. Now that was a treat! The journey

was long, often ten hours, noisy and bumpy, as we had several stops on the way, so sleep was virtually impossible for those of us too young to have had a few drinks before turning in.

Anne Pelham Burn, whose family home was in Aberdeenshire, certainly felt that sleeper trains were very much a part of her childhood:

The whole family would decamp, I think in June, to a house near Oxford for about a month. That meant four children from about 2 to 7 plus Parents, Nanny, Nursery maid, Lady's maid, Butler, Footman, Cook, Head Housemaid, Chauffeur. Everyone, plus prams and cots as needed and I presume mountains of luggage was piled onto the train in Aberdeen and off we went and returned by train a month later.

Eventually we went to school in England and travelled by sleeper always. That meant fights for the top bunks until we realised that the temperature up there could be fit for a sauna and the bottom bunks were several degrees cooler. The scratchy moquette of the bunks on which we lay, pillow provided, plus a scratchy tartan blanket of dubious cleanliness, were alleviated by my mother having bought us all some sort of cashmere or similar blankets which she turned into sleeping bags for all four of us. If we opened the window for air, smuts from the engine poured in; shut the window and we started to fry.

We were woken in the morning by the sleeping car attendants with cups of railway tea as we, yawning, approached King's Cross. Then to the King's Cross Station Hotel for breakfast after which we were met by whichever parental friend had been delegated to look after us and send us onto boarding school.

The process was reversed when we travelled home for the holidays. King's Cross, crowded with barrows looking like wooden beds on wheels, weighed down with huge pieces of luggage of all sorts, from a spare prosthesis leg belonging to a friend of our parents to fishing rods and shotguns in leather cases, their owners travelling north to enjoy Scotland in summer.

Over the years the railway engines somehow became less intriguing to me – the original ones belching clouds of steam and smoke and soot, their wheels frantically turning ever faster to bear us south or north, puffing increasingly noisily to pull their carriages uphill and then to career downwards at what seemed like suicidal speed in relative silence behind the clatter and chatter of the wheels, and always that familiar background noise of a railway engine, it's appetite for coal fed and satisfied by the stoker, going about its travelling business to the best of its ability. The noise, and the rhythm of it, finally sent us to sleep confident that all was well and that we would arrive at our destination, north or south, if not completely refreshed, at least ready to face whatever the day might bring.

The travel writer Paul Theroux has summed up the romance of the sleeping car in his book *The Great Railway Bazaar*:

The romance associated with the sleeping car derives from its extreme privacy, combining the best features of a cupboard with forward movement. Whatever drama is being enacted in this moving bedroom is heightened by the landscape passing the window: a swell of hills, the surprise of mountains, the loud metal bridge, or the melancholy sight of people standing under yellow lamps. And the notion of travel as a continuous vision, a grand tour's succession of memorable images across a curved earth – with none of the distorting emptiness of air or sea – is possible only on a train. A train is a vehicle that allows residence: dinner in the diner, nothing could be finer.

So let's sit back at our table in the lounge car, or relax on our comfortable berth, and let our minds be captured by all the exciting and romantic possibilities of the long sixteen-carriage train sitting at Platform 1 in Euston station. That sense of expectation was beautifully expressed by an American writer, Stephen Crane, in his short story 'The Scotch Express', written in 1898 but just as resonant today:

The sort of luggage trolley that would have been a common sight in Edwardian days, piled with luggage for the trip north. Photographed at the National Railway Museum, York. (Author's Collection)

Against the masonry of a platform, under a vaulted arch of the train-house, lay a long string of coaches. There were no Second Class compartments: they were all third and First Class. Presently a railway 'flier', painted a glowing vermilion, slid modestly down and took its place at the head. The guard walked along the platform and decisively closed each door. The driver turned a wheel, and as the fireman slipped back, the train moved along the platform. The crowd of porters and transient people stood respectful. This train was off for Scotland. It had started from the home of one accent to the home of another accent. It was going from manner to manner, from habit to habit, and in the minds of these London spectators there surely floated dim images of the traditional kilts, the burring speech, the grouse, the canniness, the oat-meal, all the elements of a romantic Scotland.

So all aboard the Caledonian Sleeper, hotel-on-wheels, romantic rendezvous, the journey of a night-time, where anything can happen, and probably will...

The Sleeper crossing Rannoch Moor in evening light, 3 August 2017. (Stuart Vallis)

End Piece

The poem 'At Euston by one who is not going' by A. M. Harbord is reasonably well known, with its final refrain:

Rod and guncase in the carriage,
Wise retriever in the van;
Go, and good luck travel with you!
(Wish I'd half your luck, my man!)

Less well known is this piece, along similar lines, by Alfred Cochrane, first published in *Punch* around 1920 and pointed out to me by Giles Charrington who, like me, has many happy memories of travelling on the Anglo-Scottish sleepers:

Does your heart still beat with the old excitement
As you wait where the Scotch expresses are?
Does it answer still to the old indictment
Of a fond delight in the sleeping car,
As it did when the rush through the autumn night
Meant the gate of desire ajar?

Or has the enchanting task grown tougher?
Has that arrow beyond you flown?
The hill that was once rough enough grown rougher,
The steepest climb you've ever known?
For the forest abhors a veteran duffer,
Sorely beaten and blown.

Ah, the years, the years, they are rusty and mothy;
The flesh it is weak, that once was strong.
But the brown burn over the stone falls frothy;
The music it sings is a siren song –

And the pony'll take you as far as the bothy,
And that'll help you along.

See! From the tops the mist is stealing!
Out with the stalking glass for a spy!
Round Craig an Eran an eagle is wheeling,
Black on the blue September sky.
A fig for the years! Why, youth and healing
At the end of your journey lie.

Alfred Cochrane, quoted in Annette Hope, *A Caledonian Feast* (Canongate).

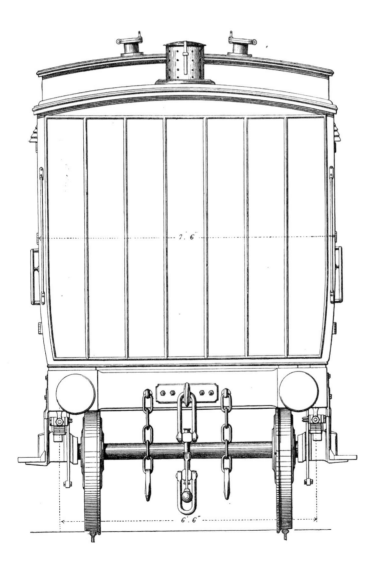

Rear view of
North British
Railway Sleeping
Carriage, 1873.